Steve Dobson

UNUSUAL HOTELS
UK & IRELAND

JONGLEZ

INTRODUCTION

"UNUSUAL HOTELS OF the UK" looks beyond the bedrooms of most chain hotels to find hotels, bed and breakfast properties as well as holiday lets that provide value-for-money memories that will last long after the bill has been paid.

From train carriages to tipis, lighthouses, historic buildings and castles, your accommodation need never again be boring. Selections are all unusual and, unlike designer properties charging stratospheric overnight rates, the only WOW factor you'll find is the property itself, not the bill.

Some might ask you to dig a little deeper for a once-in-a-lifetime experience, but the majority of properties are within reach of us all – and often cheaper than bland, corporate hotels offering little more than a bed, bath and an overpriced bar.

I hope you enjoy this selection of Unusual Hotels of the UK and Ireland and choose to "GoUnusual" for your future travels.

Steve Dobson

Our selection criteria
Properties do not pay a fee to be included in this book and are selected from the Unusual Hotels of the World website by visitors, contributors and the editorial team. This award-winning online guide includes hotels, holiday rental properties, bed and breakfast guesthouses and holiday homes. Up-to-date commentary and reviews from over 2,500 daily visitors ensure that hotel highlights are celebrated and warnings of poor experience provided.

Submit your suggestions
Comments on this book and its contents, as well as information on places we may not have mentioned, are more than welcome and will enrich future editions.
Don't hesitate to contact us:
• Jonglez publishing, 17, boulevard du Roi, 78000 Versailles, France
• E-mail: info@jonglezpublishing.com, info@uhotw.com

SOUTH WEST & CHANNEL ISLANDS

1. Fort Clonque
2. La Corbière Radio Tower
3. Nicolle Tower
4. Star Castle Hotel
5. The Egyptian House
6. Wolf Rock Lizard Lighthouse
7. Sally Port Lighthouse cottage
8. The House in the Sea
9. Cornish Tipi Holidays
10. Railholiday
11. Lundy
12. Broomhill Art Hotel
13. Pack of Cards
14. Seven Degrees West
15. Beckford's Tower
16. Grand Cru
17. White Horse Gypsy Caravans
18. White Topps Hotel

LONDON & SOUTH EAST

19. The Enchanted Manor
20. Vintage Vacations
21. Xoron Floating Hotel
22. Island Charters B&B
23. Luttrell's Tower
24. Malmaison - Oxford
25. Crazy Bear – Oxford
26. The Old Railway Station
27. Castle Cottages
28. Crazy Bear – Beaconsfield
29. Hampton Court Palace
30. Miller's Residence
31. Pavilion Hotel
32. Hotel Pelirocco
33. Sea Spray Hotel
34. Livingstone Safari Lodge
35. Lodesman, Khina Lighthouse cottages

WALES & WEST MIDLANDS

36. Caban Casita
37. The Aberporth Express
38. Gypsy Caravan and Cabin
39. North Stack
40. Black Mountain Yurt
41. The Mirador guest house
42. Portmeirion
43. Snowdonia Manor / Plas y Dduallt
44. St Curig's Church
45. The Lighthouse, Llandudno
46. Showman's Waggon
47. Cledan Valley Tipis
48. West Usk Lighthouse
49. Capel Pentwyn
50. The Citadel
51. The Summerhouse

52. The Library House
53. The Temple
54. Arley Tower

EAST MIDLANDS & EAST ANGLIA

55. Osbaston House – Feather Down Farms
56. Houseboat Hotels
57. Gothic Temple
58. The Windmill
59. The House of Correction
60. Appleton Water Tower
61. Cley Windmill
62. Freston Tower
63. The Old Methodist Chapel
64. Martello Tower
65. The House in the Clouds

NORTHERN ENGLAND

66. The Music Room
67. Hard Days Night Hotel
68. Four Winds Tipis
69. Great St John Hotel
70. Spire House
71. Beamsley Hospital
72. Culloden Tower
73. Pot-A-Doodle-Do Northumbrian Wigwams
74. The Fallen Angel
75. Straw Bale Cabin
76. La Rosa
77. Bats and Broomsticks
78. The Station House
79. The Windmill Hotel
80. RaiLeisure

SCOTLAND & IRELAND

81. Cove Park
82. Corsewall Lighthouse Hotel
83. The Hill House
84. The Mackintosh Building
85. The Pineapple
86. Liberton Tower
87. Witchery by the Castle
88. Prestonfield
89. Fernie Castle
90. The Old Station
91. Craighall Castle
92. Castle Stuart
93. The Old Church of Urquhart
94. Sleeperzzz
95. Loop Head Lightkeepers House
96. Kilvahan Horse-Drawn Caravans
97. Killiane Castle
98. Wicklow Head Lighthouse
99. Schoolhouse Hotel

● = Main Addresses   ○ = Other unusual properties in the area

INDEX

SOUTH WEST & CHANNEL ISLANDS

LONDON & SOUTH EAST

WALES & WEST MIDLANDS

EAST MIDLANDS & EAST ANGLIA

NORTHERN ENGLAND

SCOTLAND & IRELAND

N

Shetland Islands

• Lerwick

Orkney Islands

• Kirkwall

Cape Wrath

Thurso   Duncansby Head

Steornabhagh (Stornoway)   Scourie   Wick

Isle of Lewis

OUTER HEBRIDES   Ullapool

Uibhist a Tuath (North Uist)   Moray Firth

Uig   Banff

Uibhist a Deas (South Uist)   Portree   Inverness   Elgin   Peterhead

Loch Baghasdail (Lochboisdale)   Isle   Kyle of   Loch   Aviemore   Aberdeen
                                     of Skye   Lochalsh   Ness

Barra   Fort William   S c o t l a n d

Coll   Pitlochry

ATLANTIC   Tiree   Perth   Dundee   NORTH SEA

OCEAN   Isle of Mull   Oban

Colonsay   Jura   Stirling

Islay   Firth of Forth

Malin   Glasgow   Edinburgh

Head   Isle of   Berwick-upon-Tweed
                    Arran

Letterkenny   Londonderry   Dumfries

Donegal   N o r t h e r n   Carlisle   Newcastle upon Tyne
                 I r e l a n d

Ballina   Sligo   Enniskillen   Belfast   Workington   Penrith   Middlesbrough

Oileáin Acla   Boyle   Cavan   Isle of   Kendal   Scarborough
(Achill Island)
         Westport   Drogheda   Man   Douglas   Lancaster   Bridlington

Clifden   Connemara   IRISH SEA   Blackpool   Preston   York   Kingston upon Hull

         Galway   Athlone   Leeds   Grimsby

Oileáin Árann   Roscrea   Dublin   Anglesey   Liverpool   Manchester   Scunthorpe
(Aran Islands)
         Ennis   Holyhead   Sheffield   Lincoln

REP. OF IRELAND   Wicklow   Caernarfon   Stoke-   Derby   The
                                                        on-Trent   Wash

An Daingean   Kilkenny   Arklow   Cardigan   Shrewsbury   Nottingham   Norwich
(Dingle)   Bay   Leicester   Peterborough
         Limerick   Lowestoft
Killarney   Waterford   Wexford   Aberystwyth   Worcester   Birmingham   Northampton   Cambridge
                                                                                        Ipswich
         Cork   Rosslare   W a l e s   England   Bedford

Bantry   Harbour   Gloucester   Oxford   Luton   London
                Fishguard
Mizen   St David's Head   Pembroke   Newport   Bristol   Southend-on-Sea
Head
                        Swansea   Cardiff   ⑮ ⑯ ⑰   Dover
                        Bristol Channel   Portsmouth   Oostende
p. 8   ⑪   ⑬   Taunton   ⑱   Southampton   Brighton   Hastings   Dunkerque
        Bideford   ⑫   Poole   Calais
                ⑨   Exeter   Weymouth
        ⑧   Launceston   Lyme
        ⑩   Plymouth   Bay   Isle of Wight
⑤   Penzance   ⑦   Start Point   CHANNEL
Isles of Scilly   ⑥   Dieppe
④   Land's   Lizard   CHANNEL
        End   Point   ISLANDS   ①
                                Alderney
                        Guernsey   Sark   Cherbourg   Le Havre   FRANCE
                        St Peter Port   ② ③
                        Jersey

0   50   100   150   200 km

SOUTH WEST
& CHANNEL ISLANDS

FORT CLONQUE

18th-century fortified harbour defences

FORT CLONQUE ❶
Alderney

THE LANDMARK TRUST
Shottesbrooke
Maidenhead
Berkshire SL6 3SW
01628 825925
bookings@landmarktrust.org.uk
www.landmarktrust.org.uk

ROOMS AND RATES
The fort accommodates
up to thirteen people in
six bedrooms. Prices for
the whole property are
from £785 for a four-night
midweek stay in January to
£3,667 for a week in July /
August. There are frequent
flights to Alderney from
Southampton, Bournemouth
and Brighton / Shoreham.

IN THE 1840s it was thought that the advent of steam would make the Channel Islands more important as an advance naval base, and also more liable to capture by the French. Accordingly the great harbour works of Alderney were begun in 1847. Fort Clonque, the most remarkable of them, occupies a group of large rocks off the steep south-west tip of the island, commanding the passage between it and the island of Burhou. The property is reached by a causeway leading to a drawbridge entrance and was originally designed for ten 64-pounder guns in four open batteries, manned by two officers and fifty men. Before the defensive capabilities of the base were fully realized, the further development of steam brought the Channel Islands within easy reach of mainland bases, and made a base in Alderney unnecessary.

In 1886 the Defence Committee recommended that Clonque, and all the other works except Fort Albert, should be disarmed but left standing. It was thus that Hitler found them in 1940 and, imagining again that the Channel Islands had strategic value, vigorously refortified them. At Fort Clonque, part of the Victorian soldiers' quarters was replaced by an enormous casemate, housing a gun so large that its emplacement now makes a handsome bedroom looking towards Guernsey.

Most forts are large and grim, but Clonque was snugly fitted to the surrounding rocks, and is small, open and picturesque, ingeniously contrived on many levels. The fort's location will sometimes make it cold and damp, however the compensation is the delight of its spectacular setting. Views are second to none; to the lighthouses of the Casquets; colonies of gannets and seabirds that fish around the fort; and of the formidable race or current called the Swinge that runs between Clonque and Burhou.

TO DO

Alderney benefits from clean air and fresh breezes and is a peaceful and extremely pleasant island, just small enough to be explored entirely on foot or, very easily, by bikes that can be hired locally. The Victorian and German defence works are interesting, while the beaches at the north end are exceptional with plentiful, white sand. On calm days the sea can be heard all round the Clonque, restlessly searching the rocks; and on rough days it's comforting to reflect that the wall of the East Flank Battery is 19 ft thick. Stormy weather is no stranger to this location, and during some high tides the fort is cut off and the sea runs between it and the mainland.

The main town of St Anne is very pretty, English with a hint of France. There is an excellent restaurant serving local seafood in Bray. Visitors often remark that they are stepping back into a bygone age of friendly people, good pubs and a more relaxed pace of life.

VISITOR COMMENTS
• *Rarely have I felt so relaxed or comfortable and been somewhere so beautiful.*
• *The cycling on Alderney is fabulous.*

LA CORBIÈRE RADIO TOWER

Second World War observation tower relic, converted for residential use

JERSEY HERITAGE ❷
The Weighbridge
St Helier
Jersey JE2 3NF
01534 633304
heritagelets@
jerseyheritagetrust.org
www.jerseyheritagetrust.org

ROOMS AND RATES
The property sleeps six in three bedrooms. Outside the main summer season, three-night short breaks cost £490. In 2009, a week-long rental in high season is £1,560. As the accommodation is spread over six floors there are a number or steps. These are particularly steep up to the top-level living area. Children should be closely supervised near the tower due to its cliff-top location.

LOCATION
Overlooking Corbière lighthouse on Jersey's south-west coast, the property has a double garage adjoining the building so you can use your own car or choose to take advantage of the buses to visit the attractions of Jersey.

DURING THE OCCUPATION of Jersey during the Second World War, three huge observation towers were built by the Germans as part of Hitler's Atlantic Wall defences. Their purpose was to direct artillery fire against targets out to sea. One of these, La Corbière Radio Tower, now provides accommodation. Constructed from more than 5,000 bags of cement, this is a truly imposing site from both land and sea. It commands excellent views over Jersey, the Gulf of St Malo and Corbière Lighthouse, which stands on an outcrop of beautiful pink granite rocks just offshore. The lighthouse was once manned but is now remotely operated – however the light still shines at night and during fog you can't escape the fog horn. Bring earplugs, just in case! You can walk to the lighthouse along a causeway during low tide.

From the tower's rather functional beginning comes accommodation that is unique to Jersey. The tower has six floors and the first three are identical, with a double bedroom and shower / toilet on each floor. The climb to the top room is more than worth the effort. The look-out centre that was once the heart of the tower's activity now offers a jaw-dropping 360° view that must be seen to be believed, converted into a stunning living / dining area that is as stylish as it is spectacular.

Three shower rooms (with toilet), a kitchen, cloakroom and three fitted double bedrooms have been created out of the eight rooms that lead up to the tower centre. The upstairs living area is heated and has CD / DVD player, TV, fridge and binoculars. There is an electric oven and four rings, plus underfloor heating in bedrooms, kitchen and shower rooms.

NICOLLE TOWER

Navigation tower and lookout

NICOLLE TOWER ❸
St Clement's, Jersey

THE LANDMARK TRUST
Shottesbrooke
Maidenhead
Berkshire SL6 3SW
01628 825925
bookings@landmarktrust.org.uk
www.landmarktrust.org.uk

ROOMS AND RATES
With a single bedroom
for two, this cosy
landmark offers a unique
perspective of the island
and its surroundings.
Prices for the whole
property are from £119 for
a four-night midweek break
in January, to £937 for a
week in July / August.
The staircase is necessarily
steep without access for
disabled guests. The tower
also provides a garden should
you tire of bird's-eye views.

THIS 160 FT navigational mark is located in a field called Le Clos de Hercanty, where Hercanty means "tilted menhir". Used as a navigation mark, a small rectangular lookout was built next to the stone. In 1644, this half-buried slab of diorite was marked with a compass rose inscription to become part of the foundations of a new lookout building, forming one corner. Records indicate that 18th-century owner Philippe Nicolle added the octagonal sitting room on the first floor in 1821. Further work was undertaken in 1943 by the occupying forces of the German army. They made an observation or control position here by astutely raising the roof of the octagon by a single storey so that no change would be noticed from the air. Although this latest addition with its slit eyes and German ranging marks on its thick concrete ceiling isn't part of the original tower, it has been renovated as part of the tower's history.

TO DO
Set back from the coast, 160 ft up, the tower provides endlessly fascinating views over the sea and island in every direction.

VISITOR COMMENTS
• *Peace, lovely walks, our own tower to live in — what more could you want?*

THE EGYPTIAN HOUSE

Celebration of Napoleonic success in Egypt

THE EGYPTIAN HOUSE ❺
Chapel Street,
Penzance, Cornwall

THE LANDMARK TRUST
Shottesbrooke
Maidenhead
Berkshire SL6 3SW
01628 825925
bookings@landmarktrust.org.uk
www.landmarktrust.org.uk

ROOMS AND RATES
Three apartments. The
first floor with a narrow
oval staircase to negotiate
accommodates up to three.
The second and third floors
accommodate up to four each
in double and twin rooms.
Prices for the whole
property are from £110 for
a four-night midweek break
in January, to £707 for a
week in July / August.

OF A STYLE in vogue after Napoleon's campaign in Egypt of 1798, The Egyptian house dates from about 1835. The front elevation is very similar to that of the former Egyptian Hall in Piccadilly, designed in 1812 by P. F. Robinson. Robinson or Foulston of Plymouth are the most likely candidates for its design, although there is no evidence to support the claim of either. It was built for John Lavin as a museum and geological repository. Bought by The Landmark Trust 1968, its colossal façade, with lotus-bud capitals and enrichments of Coade stone, concealed two small granite houses above shops, solid and with a pleasant rear elevation, but very decrepit inside. These were reconstructed into three compact apartments, the highest of which has a view through a small window of Mounts Bay and St Michael's Mount, over the chimney pots of the city.

VISITOR COMMENTS

• *No photograph or drawing can depict the astonishing and eccentric elevation of the Egyptian house.*

• *We much appreciated the furniture and delighted in the witty Egyptian motifs.*

WOLF ROCK – LIZARD LIGHTHOUSE

The most southerly point of mainland UK

CORNISH COTTAGES LTD ⬛
Mullion Meadows
Mullion
Helston
Cornwall TR12 7HB
01326 240333
www.cornishcottagesonline.com

ROOMS AND RATES

The lighthouse is owned by Trinity House, which now works with Cornish Cottages Ltd to manage the lettings for this location, following recent restoration of the six different lighthouse keeper cottages at Lizard Point. Sleeping six in a king, double and twin beds, the property can be rented on a self-catering basis from £416 in low winter season to £1,126 in high summer. One of the bedrooms is downstairs with an en suite shower room. Also on the ground floor are the kitchen and family bathroom. The downstairs lounge is the base of the disused twin of the lighthouse, and has a fantastic sea view. Upstairs in the main cottage are a further two bedrooms. Rental includes bed linen, towels, electricity, central heating, cot and highchair. No dogs or smoking are allowed and children must be supervised at all times.

LOCATION

You are just 1/4 mile from Lizard village with its pub, shops and restaurants.

LIZARD LIGHTHOUSE IS positioned at the southernmost tip of mainland UK and offers a number of lighthouse keeper's cottages providing a coastal view – just a few yards from the front door. The working lighthouse was established in 1619, with the current towers being built in 1752. In 1924 it became the first electrically powered lighthouse before being fully automated in 1998 with a 26 mile light range and an automatic 3 mile fog signal if conditions are misty.

"Wolf Rock" is the first of the lighthouse cottages at the west end and incorporates the unused West Tower as part of the accommodation. The circular floor of the tower is the dining room, off which thirty-two stone spiral steps lead you upwards to the "observatory". Here a quiet seating area provides tranquility, or stand at the windows for a breathtaking 180° view around Lizard Point.

TO DO

There is an on-site visitor centre providing tours of the working lighthouse and an opportunity to learn about the work of Trinity House, however it is unlikely that the number of visitors will affect your privacy. While the scenery is dramatic for walking, The Lizard also has a number of nearby coves and sandy beaches.

SALLY PORT COTTAGE

Setting for children's TV show "Fraggle Rock"

SALLY PORT COTTAGE ❼
St Mawes, Cornwall

RURAL RETREATS
Draycott Business Park
Draycott
Moreton-in-Marsh
Gloucestershire GL56 9JY
01386 701177
www.ruralretreats.co.uk

ROOMS AND RATES
The lighthouse is owned by Trinity House and bookings are managed by Rural Retreats on their behalf. Sally Port Cottage is a single dwelling with a sitting room, kitchen and en suite master bedroom on the ground floor. The double bed can be converted into two single beds if required. There is also a small twin bedroom, bathroom with separate shower and toilet. Outdoor furniture is provided to take advantage of the patio sun-trap. Separate from the main building, the detached observation room overlooks the sea. No dogs, no smoking, and due to the proximity to dangerous cliff edges, no babies or children under 14 years are permitted. The minimum booking for four guests in low winter season is two nights with pricing from £368. In high summer season the minimum is seven nights and pricing is from £1,598 on a self-catering basis.

ALL LIGHTHOUSES PROVIDE an opportunity to unwind because of their situation, either basking in the sunshine as you look out to sea, or cosy within heavy masonry in storms and adverse conditions. As well as this maritime role, St Anthony's lighthouse was the base for the British TV version of children's programme Fraggle Rock, created by Jim Henson (of Muppets fame) and syndicated worldwide in the mid-1980s.

The cottage is totally private with no public access. There is an observation room with a large picture window, table, chairs and an electric wood-effect stove so that you can be snug while watching the worst of any storms.

You are reminded that St Anthony's is an operational lighthouse. There is an electronic fog signal that operates automatically, so ear plugs are provided ...

TO DO

There are numerous places of interest to visit nearby, notably the Eden Project, the Lost Gardens of Heligan, and historic Truro, the capital of Cornwall. The restaurant at The Driftwood Hotel (Portscatho – 3 miles) is highly recommended and accepts bookings from non-residents. Afternoon tea at the Tresanton Hotel in nearby St Mawes is recommended, as is the Fish and Chips Night (Friday) at the Rising Sun. The surrounding National Trust land has wonderful walks and a bird hide which is a 10 minute walk away, from where you can watch peregrine falcons nest, along with many other heathland and coastal birds.

RAILHOLIDAY

Restored railway carriages offering self-catering accommodation in two locations

RAILHOLIDAY ❿
Haparanda Station
Nut Tree Hill
St Germans
Cornwall PL12 5LU
01503 230783
daveandlizzy@railholiday.co.uk
www.railholiday.co.uk

ROOMS AND RATES
At St Germans, The Old Luggage Van sleeps four and The Travelling Post Office sleeps six, while The St Ives Bay at Hayle is split into two units that can accommodate two families using separate entrances or larger groups of eight to twelve. Prices vary according to location and season, with a summer week in The Old Luggage Van from £496.

LOCATION
The picturesque village of St Germans is in an Area of Outstanding Natural Beauty and has a well-stocked shop and pub with a good food reputation. It is 2 miles from the A38 main road. Hayle is on the west coast of Cornwall, 5 miles from St Ives.

RAILHOLIDAY IS A family company that has built a living providing self-catering accommodation in restored railway carriages. The family started with the restoration of The Old Luggage Van in 1995 and such was the demand that they added The Travelling Post Office to their St Germans station base. They have since added The St Ives Bay SK2 carriage at their second location in Hayle, about 5 miles from St Ives on the west coast of Cornwall.

Each carriage has a different character, and perhaps the most historic is the 48 ft long Travelling Post Office No. 841, built for the Great Western Railway. It went into service in 1889, hauled by the City of Truro on its famous 100 mph run and was originally designed for broad gauge running. Converted to standard gauge in 1891 until its withdrawal in 1934, for many years the carriage formed part of a house in Wales. Now converted to sleep up to six in a combination of double room, sofa bed and bunk beds, The Travelling Post Office is a great place for families, friends and couples alike.

The passenger luggage van also has seen long service, having been built for the London and South Western Railway (LSWR) at Eastleigh in 1896. It was recovered from a site at Wadebridge, Cornwall, in 1995 following its withdrawal from service in August 1932.

What the St Ives Bay carriage might lack in history (it was built in 1957), it makes up in original fittings, including all the compartments, lamp shades, luggage racks, mirrors, blinds and upholstery.

LUNDY ISLAND

A preserved castle, lighthouse and cottages on this nature reserve island

LUNDY ISLAND ⑪
Bristol Channel, Devon

DETAILS
There are a variety of
overnight options including
cottages, a hostel and even
camping. The twenty-three
houses and cottages include
some built around the keep
of the castle, the keeper's
quarters of the lighthouse
and a stone refuge without
electricity – "Tibbets", which
has its own rustic charm.
Between March and
November, The Landmark
Trust runs a ferry from
Bideford or Ilfracombe
carrying day and overnight
visitors, weather permitting.
Autumn and winter access
is by helicopter from
Hartland Point. Prices
vary according to the type
of accommodation.

THE LANDMARK TRUST
Shottesbrooke
Maidenhead
Berkshire SL6 3SW
01628 825925
bookings@landmarktrust.org.uk
www.landmarktrust.org.uk

LUNDY ("PUFFIN ISLAND"), in the approaches to the Bristol Channel, is 3 miles long and rises over 400 ft out of the sea, commanding a tremendous view of England, Wales and the Atlantic. It has tall cliffs towards the south and west, with grass and heather on top, and steep side lands with trees, shrubs and bracken in small hanging valleys, rich in wild-flowers, on the east coast facing the mainland. There are three lighthouses (two in use), a castle, a church, a working farm, a pub, several handsome houses and cottages, and a population of about eighteen. Most of the buildings and all the field walls are made from the island's beautiful light-coloured granite.

When Lundy was taken on by The National Trust in 1969 (thanks mainly to the generosity of Sir Jack Hayward), The Landmark Trust undertook the restoration and running of the island. The formidable task of tidying up and restoring the buildings and services for both visitors and residents took them over twenty years. Much of this work remains invisible, but without it ordinary people would soon have been unable to live on or visit the island.

TO DO

Lundy offers the public a very rare experience. It is large enough to have a genuine life of its own, which visitors can share and enjoy, but small and far enough away to be a world apart and undefaced. There is rock climbing and diving for the energetic, bird watching and enjoying unspoilt nature for those more contemplative. All visitors have free run of the island to sample both the pleasures of escape and participation: walks or wanderings high up, in the silence, looking east across the blue floor of the sea to the coast of Devon, or westward over the limitless Atlantic; or sociable visits to the tavern and shop.

VISITOR COMMENTS

• *All islands have their peculiarities. Some possess a unique light, or exude their own scent. Lundy however displays a more intrinsic element, which can be simply described as a shortage of time. It is partly this commodity that makes Lundy precious.*

BROOMHILL ART HOTEL

B&B hotel with art gallery, sculpture garden and restaurant

BROOMHILL ART HOTEL ⑫
Muddiford Road
Barnstaple
Devon EX31 4EX
01271 850 262
info@broomhillart.co.uk
www.broomhillart.co.uk

ROOMS AND RATES
There are six rooms and
a two-bedroom cottage
for four available.
Stays for Friday and Saturday
on a half-board basis are £215
for a double room including
a three-course dinner.
Broomhill also offers a £100
"Lunch and Stay" package
for Tuesday, Wednesday and
Thursday which includes one
night in an en suite room,
lunch in the Broomhill
restaurant, English breakfast
and free admission to
the sculpture garden.

LOCATION
Broomhill is just north
of Barnstaple in North
Devon. From Barnstaple,
take the A39 towards
Lynton, then left onto the
B3230 towards Ilfracombe.
Broomhill is signposted 2
miles after the hospital.

SINCE OPENING IN 1997, Broomhill Art Hotel has offered overnight guests access to the 10 acre sculpture park which showcases 300 contemporary sculptures by over sixty sculptors. The park is surrounded by hundreds of acres of North Devon woodland and is bounded by its own stream. As well as sculptures outside, the hotel has a gallery and works of art around the house to enjoy. Many of the works of art, statues and bronzes on display are available to purchase.

The property itself is a late Victorian period property with six light and airy en suite rooms decorated with antiques and a private art collection. Bed and breakfast bookings are available from Sunday to Thursday and half-board on Friday and Saturday. Food is from their organic restaurant, winner of the North Devon Good Food Award. Broomhill also organizes jazz with tapas concerts in the next door art gallery. Often sold out, early booking is recommended.

TO DO
Located only 2 miles from Barnstaple, Broomhill is within easy reach of the sandy beaches of Woolacombe, Exmoor and the beautiful North Devon countryside.

SEVEN DEGREES WEST

Restored VW camper vans for hire

SEVEN DEGREES WEST ⓮
7 Dalston Road
Southville
Bristol, BS3 1QQ
0117 904 4987
info@sevendegreeswest.co.uk
www.sevendegreeswest.co.uk

RATES AND INFORMATION
Vans sleep four comfortably,
and two more in the
external awning.
Low season rates
(November–March) are
£300 for a weekend, rising
to £400 between April
and October. A seven-day
rental in high season is
around £100 a night. The
fee includes comprehensive
insurance, breakdown cover
and unlimited mileage.
7°W are concerned about
the environmental impact
of their business and plant
a tree on your behalf
for every trip using
www.carbonfootprint.com,
as part of the rental price.

DETAILS
Leave your own car, free
of charge, at their secure
warehouse during your trip.
Alternatively, the team can
meet you at Bristol airport,
rail or coach station, or
anywhere within a 15 mile
radius of their Bristol base.
By prior arrangement and
fee, they can organize the
valeting and MoT of your
car while you're away too!

WHAT BETTER WAY to see England than in a classic type II Volkswagen camper van, imported brand new from VW Brazil. Equipped to a high specification, you can ride in style with the 7°W fleet – Cromarty, Rockall, Malin or Dogger. Providing lowered suspension for improved handling, alloy wheels and chrome bumpers, they combine reliability with fabulous traditional retro looks.

Inside you can seat three in the front on a bench seat and three in the back. The rear seat converts to a king-size double bed. There is also a double bed in the raisable roof which is perfect for fun with family or friends. You have the option of a drive-away awning should you wish for additional space.

There is a stove and small fitted fridge, plus a sink with electric pumped cold water. A buddy seat in the back allows dining for four. Each van comes with crockery / cutlery and a CD/iPod stereo dock. Waiting in your van when you pick up will be a welcome pack of maps and guides to whatever area you're going and things you may need for that all-important first-morning camping breakfast.

Mains hook-up connects you to power on campsites and independent blown-air heating gives you the freedom to travel all year round, secure in the knowledge that you'll have a warm, dry place to spend your holiday.

TO DO
Run by father and son team Andrew and Ben Purcell, 7°W are approachable and brimming with enthusiasm and suggestions for road trip destinations. Whether you're heading to Cornwall, Devon, Dorset or the west coast of Wales, as a single camper van or convoy of four vans with twenty-four friends, the team share their growing database of campsite, attraction and activity ideas and recommendations.

BECKFORD'S TOWER

Artistic tower folly in historic city location

BECKFORD'S TOWER ⓯
Lansdown Road, Bath

ROOMS AND RATES
The tower accommodates
up to four individuals in
two bedrooms with a small
garden and adjacent parking.
Prices for the whole
property are from £321 for
a four-night midweek break
in January, to £1,222 for a
week in July / August.
The museum and the tower
(but not the accommodation)
are open to the public
on weekends and Bank
Holiday Mondays from
10.30 am–5.00 pm between
Easter and October.
bookings@landmarktrust.org.uk
www.landmarktrust.org.uk

THE LANDMARK TRUST
Shottesbrooke
Maidenhead
Berkshire SL6 3SW
01628 825925

THIS TOWER, COMMISSIONED by William Beckford (1760–1844), is designed in a Greek revival style with a hint of Tuscany. Born immensely rich, Beckford became a collector, patron, writer and eccentric builder. Cold-shouldered by English society, he became a recluse and bought two adjacent houses in Bath's Lansdown Road, to pursue his fascination with towers.

Each morning, accompanied by his dwarf and pack of spaniels, Beckford would ride up to his tower to play with his treasures in its opulent rooms, described in the books of the tower museum, displayed on the first floor.

After Beckford's death the tower became a chapel and its grounds an elegant cemetery. Now restored and converted into flats, the ground floor is available to let.

TO DO

This property has been restored to recreate the layout and something of the flavour of Beckford's interiors, especially in the sumptuous Scarlet Drawing Room. Like him, those who stay here can climb the fine spiral staircase to the "Belvedere" just below the elaborate, gilded lantern and enjoy, all to themselves, what Beckford called "the finest prospect in Europe".

VISITOR COMMENTS

• *A beautifully presented building with a lot of magic.*

SUGGESTIONS TO CHECK OUT
WHEN YOU CHECK IN

The House in the Sea, see opposite page

STAR CASTLE HOTEL ④

This Elizabethan fortress commands magnificent views of the Isles of Scilly. The Built in 1593 in the form of an eight-pointed star, there are eight rooms in the main castle, three on the ramparts and twenty-seven rooms in the garden area. Be prepared for an uphill walk to the Star Castle hotel, which is at the top of the town.
• Prices are from £136 per person per night on a dinner, bed and breakfast half-board basis.
Star Castle Hotel, St Mary's, Isles of Scilly TR21 0TA • 01720 422317 • www.star-castle.co.uk

THE HOUSE IN THE SEA ⑧

Across a 70 ft-high suspension bridge
This two-bedroom property is located on a rock on Towan Beach in Newquay and guests must cross a 70 ft-high suspension bridge to reach it.
• Double room £160, single £160.
• **Newquay Island** Coastal Retreat, Newquay, Cornwall TR7 1EA • 01637 879754

CORNISH TIPI HOLIDAYS ⑨

Launched in 1997 and providing some of the first tipis in the UK, this forty-tipi site has a fantastic following and offers a relaxed, organized site, with flush toilets and hot showers. Tipis are in secluded groups and available in small (two-person), medium (four to five adults) and extra large (sleeping six to ten).• **Tregeare**, Pendoggett, St Kew, Cornwall PL30 3LW • 01208 880781
• www.cornishtipiholidays.co.uk

PACK OF CARDS ⑬

A house that symbolizes the features of a pack of cards
History suggests that in 1690, local councillor George Ley commemorated a large gambling win by having a new house built to symbolize the features of a pack of cards. It has four floors, to represent the four suits, thirteen rooms for the number of cards in a suit, fifty-two windows, fifty-two steps on the stairs and was supposedly built on an area measuring 52 sq. ft. Now a B&B, it is less than 10 minutes from the sea and an ideal base from which to visit Exmoor and North Devon.
• Double room £55, single £32.50.

• **High Street**, Combe Martin, Devon EX34 0ET
• 01271 882300 • www.packocards.co.uk

GRAND CRU ⑯

Two cabins in a houseboat
The Grand Cru houseboat offers two self-contained cabins with ingredients in the kitchen fridge for a self-catering breakfast.
• Six people £399, four people £359.
• **Grand Cru,** 74 Warminster Road, Bath, Somerset BA2 6RU • 01225 312935
• www.bedandbreakfastonaboat.co.uk

WHITE HORSE GYPSY CARAVANS ⑰

Relax and enjoy the rolling Wiltshire countryside in a traditional horse-drawn caravan. The gentle pace of your horse is a fantastic way to unwind and enjoy the thatched cottages, villages and country pubs of England.
• A two-berth caravan is £450 for a three-night break.• **Kate's Cottages,** Alton Priors, Marlborough, Wiltshire SN8 4JX • 01672 851119
• www.whitehorsegypsycaravans.co.uk

WHITE TOPPS HOTEL ⑱

Only with your dog
When owner Marjorie Titchen opened her seven-bedroom B&B she decided that the best way to meet people that she would get along with was to only accept dog owners as guests. All residents must therefore bring a dog with them to be able to stay. Dogs are allowed in all the rooms and there is no restriction on size, breed or the number of dogs guests can bring. • Double room £78, single £39. • **White Topps Hotel,** 45 Church Road, Southbourne, Bournemouth, Dorset BH6 4BB
• 01202 428868 • www.whitetopps.co.uk

N

Shetland Islands
• Lerwick

Orkney Islands
Kirkwall
Cape
Wrath
Thurso   • Duncansby Head
Scourie   • Wick
Steornabhagh
(Stornoway)
Isle of Lewis
OUTER HEBRIDES
Uibhist a Tuath (North Uist)   Ullapool   Moray
Uig   Firth
Uibhist a Deas (South Uist)   Portree   Inverness   Elgin   Banff
Loch Baghasdail (Lochboisdale) Isle   Loch   • Peterhead
Barra   of Skye Kyle of   Ness Aviemore
Lochalsh   • Aberdeen
Coll   Fort William   Scotland
Tiree   Pitlochry
Isle of Mull   Oban   Perth   Dundee
Colonsay   Stirling
Jura   Firth of Forth
Islay   Edinburgh
Isle of   Glasgow   Berwick-upon-Tweed
Arran

ATLANTIC
OCEAN   NORTH SEA

Malin
Head
Letterkenny
Donegal   Londonderry   Dumfries   Newcastle upon Tyne
Northern   Stranraer Solway   Carlisle
Ballina   Sligo   Ireland   Workington Firth   Penrith   Middlesbrough
Oileain Acla   Enniskillen Belfast   Scarborough
(Achill Island)   Boyle Cavan   Isle of   Kendal   Bridlington
Westport   Man   Douglas   York   Kingston upon Hull
Clifden Connemara   Drogheda   Lancaster   Grimsby
Galway Athlone   IRISH SEA   Blackpool Preston   Scunthorpe
Oileain Árann Roscrea   Dublin   Anglesey Liverpool Manchester Sheffield Lincoln
(Aran Islands) Ennis   Wicklow   Holyhead Caernarfon Stoke- Derby Nottingham The
Limerick Kilkenny Arklow   on-Trent   Wash
An Daingean REP. OF IRELAND   Shrewsbury Leicester Peterborough Norwich
(Dingle) Killarney Waterford Wexford   Aberystwyth Worcester Birmingham Northampton Cambridge Lowestoft
Bantry Cork Rosslare Cardigan Wales Gloucester England Bedford Ipswich
Harbour Bay   p. 42
Fishguard   Oxford ㉔ Luton
Mizen St David's Head Newport Bristol   ㉕   ㉘ London   Southend-on-Sea Oosten
Head Pembroke Swansea Cardiff Bristol Channel   ㉙ ㉚㉛   ㉟ Dunkerque
Bideford   Taunton   ㉖ Dover Calais
Launceston Exeter   Southampton Portsmouth ㉗ ㉝ ㉜ ㉞
Penzance Plymouth Poole ㉓   Brighton Hastings
Isles of Scilly Land's Lizard Lyme ㉒ ㉑ FRANCE
End Point Start Point Bay Weymouth ⑲ Isle of Wight
            ㉒
CHANNEL   ⑲
ISLANDS   CHANNEL   Dieppe
Guernsey Sark
St Peter Port Alderney Cherbourg   Le Havre FRANCE
Jersey

0 50 100 150 200 km

LONDON
& SOUTH EAST

THE ENCHANTED MANOR

A magical boutique retreat providing enchanted accommodation

THE ENCHANTED MANOR ❶⑨
St Catherine's point
Sandrock road
Niton
Isle of Wight PO38 2NG
01983 730215
info@enchantedmanor.co.uk
www.enchantedmanor.co.uk

LOCATION AND RATES
Within 10 minutes' drive are
the main coastal resorts of
Shanklin, Ventnor and the
island's capital, Newport.
Maggie and Ric offer
three-night weekend
packages on a B&B basis for
£275 per person, inclusive
of car ferry transfers.
Their midweek packages
are the same price, but offer
the fourth night free.

WINNER OF THE 2008 award for the UK's Funkiest B&B, a magical boutique retreat has been created by Ric and Maggie Hilton on the Isle of Wight. The Enchanted Manor is a secluded hideaway for discerning guests fed up with run-of-the-mill accommodation. It's a destination for those looking for somewhere with first-class facilities, excellent service, a friendly atmosphere, all enveloped in beautiful surroundings.

The property is decorated with the work of artist Josephine Wall and suites have hand-carved four-poster beds with comfortable bedding. The bathrooms have deluxe power showers or, if you prefer to soak, roll-top baths. Health and beauty treatments are available to pamper guests, and there is an outside pool to use in the summer months.

Within a few minutes' walk is one of the most famous and historic inns on the Isle of Wight – The Buddle. Not only does it provide a country ambience, it also offers excellent food. If you prefer, ask Maggie for a gourmet picnic to enjoy in the gardens, otherwise Aussie Ric, who knows all about barbeques, can arrange a pack of locally produced meat to cook on the BBQ provided in the gardens.

With its 5-star Gold Award from the English Tourist Board, this is a cosy, comfortable and peaceful place to stay – with warm, friendly hosts keen to make your stay enjoyable. Unsurprisingly, it is very much in demand for weddings and honeymoons.

TO DO

Located in private gardens and woodlands on the Isle of Wight, in summer evenings you can watch the family of badgers stroll the gardens, see red squirrels scurrying up the trees and enjoy the array of other wildlife that roam the grounds. Winter visits might include a stroll to see the rugged coastline and view the famous St Catherine's lighthouse a few minutes' walk away. Some of the best walks on the island are nearby, with stunning scenery, breathtaking countryside and sea views to take in. The quaint village of Niton takes you back in time with a variety of old-world shops to browse around. You'll find The Enchanted Manor a gateway to the stunning coastal drive from Niton to Freshwater Bay and a base from which to discover the beauty of the Isle of Wight.

VINTAGE VACATIONS

Vintage Airstream caravans – restored and adored

VINTAGE VACATIONS **20**
Near Newport
Isle of Wight
07802 758113
anything@
vintagevacations.co.uk
www.vintagevacations.co.uk

LOCATION AND RATES
Newport is a 10
minute drive away.
2008 weekly bookings in
high summer are £495
for a trailer of up to four
guests, with reduced rates
for low season, midweek
and weekend breaks.
Gas, water, electricity,
towels and all linen are
included. Now with ten
caravans on offer, the
site books up quickly.
To preserve these works
of art, the caravans are
non-smoking throughout and
pets are not admitted on site.

STARTING WITH A single Airstream caravan bought on eBay in 2004 as a weekend escape from London, Helen Carey saw the opportunity to offer these icons of travelling hospitality to others. Located on a dairy farm campsite, the first of these 60s and 70s works of aluminium art were brought to the Isle of Wight from Missouri and enhanced with a treasure trove of furnishings and period decor from Helen's stylist background. From melamine plates to retro print fabrics, Helen and partner Frazer have shared a stockpile of period artefacts to make the Vintage Vacation experience a hazy trip down memory lane – full of a sense of period fun.

Modern conveniences such as fridges and CD players are hidden behind the vintage exteriors so you can enjoy yourself without sacrifice. They even include a hairdryer and toaster! Some of the larger models have enough space for travel cots. The campsite has a beach hut with proper toilet facilities as you can't use the toilets on board. Once inside your Airstream you'll easily understand why they are still considered king of the road for luxury camping.

Caravans sleep up to four, however two-person tents are available to hire on site for noisy children or larger families. Helen notes that guests are "More bohemian than bog standard".

To keep everything as original as possible, Vintage Vacations have stayed with the USA voltage. This means that each trailer has its own transformer to convert UK power supply to US. There is a travel adaptor on board. Some devices such as iPods and certain DVD players and phone chargers will work, but not all, so bring a couple of favourite CDs just in case.

LUTTRELL'S TOWER

Georgian tower with views of the Solent and smugglers access tunnel

LUTTRELL'S TOWER ❷❸
Eaglehurst, Southampton,
Hampshire

THE LANDMARK TRUST
Shottesbrooke
Maidenhead
Berkshire SL6 3SW
01628 825925
bookings@landmarktrust.org.uk
www.landmarktrust.org.uk

ROOMS AND RATES
Accommodation for up to
four in a double and twin
bedroom combination.
Prices for the whole
property are from £481 for
a four-night midweek break
in January to £2,357 for a
week in July / August.

THIS GEORGIAN FOLLY, possibly the only surviving work of Thomas Sandby, first professor of architecture at the Royal Academy, stands on the shore of the Solent looking towards Cowes. The view, particularly of ships entering and leaving Southampton by the deep-water channel, is endlessly fascinating. Giant ships, sailing and pleasure craft of all shapes and sizes travel along this busy waterway and home of sailing. The view from the opposite windows of the Fawley refinery and power station is in its own way equally impressive, with miles of complex pipework knitted together in an intricate sculpture.

The tower was built for Temple Luttrell, an MP who gained a reputation locally as a smuggler, perhaps because of a tunnel running from the basement to the beach. His brother-in-law, Lord Cavan, who commanded British forces in Egypt from 1801, was the next owner and brought with him the two mysterious feet on a plinth of Nubian granite, now at the tower and thought to be the base of a XIXth dynasty statue of Rameses II. The tower had several owners, including for a time Marconi, who used it for his wireless experiments of 1912.

Purchased by The Landmark Trust in 1968 and restored to its former splendour, all the rooms have handsome chimney-pieces and the top room has fine plaster and shellwork as well. This top room has been arranged with an open-plan kitchen so that you can cook, eat and relax in it, watching the Solent all the while.

TO DO

With a roof terrace for summer months or al fresco breakfast, the real pleasure is to sit and watch. With the open spaces and walks of the New Forest nearby, this is a splendid base from which to enjoy walks and country pubs. Even in winter, the clear skies and marvellous sunsets make this a magical location.

VISITOR COMMENTS

• *A beautiful and tranquil place. We have enjoyed every minute of it.*

CRAZY BEAR – OXFORD

Flamboyance and extravagance in a country setting

CRAZY BEAR HOTEL **25**
Bear Lane
Stadhampton
Oxfordshire OX44 7UR
01865 890714
enquiries@crazybear-
oxford.co.uk
www.crazybeargroup.co.uk

RATES AND LOCATION
Seventeen rooms with
doubles from £125 per room
per night and suites up to
£400, including tax. The
hotel is down country lanes
on the outskirts of Oxford,
which is only an hour from
London or Birmingham.

THIS WAS NO ordinary pub conversion! Reception is a lavishly restyled London Routemaster double-decker bus, so you know you're in for something different from the outset.

Tropical gardens lead you to the heart of the hotel – originally a 16th-century building that has been bravely re-designed to house the charismatic bar with its 8 ft bear in a chandeliered gallery. Garden paths wander past a waterfall, dense palm trees, terraces, lawns and eye-catching art scattered throughout the grounds.

A total of seventeen individually designed bedrooms, suites and cottages showcase amazing creativity and charisma, with real wow-factor. Elaborate furniture, mirrors and beautifully crafted, sumptuous leather provide eclectic drama. The cottages can cater for families and groups of up to six, while the suites and rooms are more in keeping with a luxury romantic break for two.

Award-winning dining is another feature of the hotel. From the vibrant bar, you walk past the bear down to a Thai brasserie in a dramatic haven of its own. Royal Thai cuisine is prepared using produce from the hotel's farm and direct from Thailand. Equally sumptuous, The English restaurant envelops you in padded leather and offers modern British food.

Private dinners, weddings and meetings can take place in a rich oak room, a garden log cabin or a huge Moroccan glasshouse that opens to terraces, croquet lawn and a private copse. All of this is set at the front of 60 acres of farmland, home to rare breed animals and The Crazy Bear Farm Shop which rears, butchers, cures and smokes its own produce for the hotel.

TO DO

Oxford is only 15 minutes away by car and is a must-see. In summer, punting on the river is fantastic fun, perhaps with a change of clothing in case you fall in! The history of Oxford is retold in the many tours running all year round, and there is now a bus tour taking in the main sites.

Other local attractions include Blenheim Palace, Wittenham Clumps, historic Dorchester Abbey, the River Thames and Bicester Village designer outlet.

The hotel can arrange almost any activity in the area, including hot-air ballooning, helicopter rides, horse riding, quad biking and clay-pigeon shooting, as well as spectacular weddings and parties.

VISITOR COMMENTS

"Crazy Bear Oxford has a unique design and offers a lot of fun"

THE OLD RAILWAY STATION

Pullman carriage luxury accommodation

THE OLD RAILWAY STATION ㉖
Petworth
West Sussex GU28 0JF
01798 342346
info@old-station.co.uk
www.old-station.co.uk

ROOMS AND RATES
There are eight railway carriage suites and midweek breaks are from £107 per room, with weekend prices in summer for the most luxurious Pullman up to £176. The station house is also beautifully restored and offers rooms from £92. There is a minimum two-night stay during weekends and it's worth checking availability for midweek package offers.

LOCATION
Petworth is 10 miles from Midhurst on the South Downs, around 45 minutes by car from Gatwick airport.

PROVIDING EIGHT SUITES in restored Orient Express Pullman carriages as well as rooms in the original station house, The Old Railway Station is a landmark of rail-lover accommodation.

Luxury train journeys were once defined by the Orient Express with their Pullman carriages and four examples have been lovingly restored here. Some elements have been improved – they now have working central heating, while others have simply been retained – such as the splendour of the decorations.

It is not impossible to imagine yourself returning to the heyday of steam and The Old Railway Station provides a perfect overnight stop if you're planning to participate in nearby themed events such as the historic Goodwood Revival motorsport weekend. Anniversaries would have a touch of class here, especially if you choose to do the right thing and dress appropriately for the occasion, as would have been required in a Pullman.

TO DO

While there is no restaurant, breakfast is either served in the station building or presented to your suite. A busy local pub is 5 minutes' walk away, offering traditional ales and food, while other pubs and restaurants are close by. Petworth is handy for day trips to the south coast, including towns such as Arundel with its castle. Goodwood is also a short drive away, both for motorsport events and horse racing.

CASTLE COTTAGE B&B AND TREEHOUSE

Treehouse, cottage and barn surrounded by ancient woodland

CASTLE COTTAGE B&B **27**
Coates Castle
Fittleworth
West Sussex RH20 1EU
01798 865001
alison@castlecottage.info
www.castlecottage.info

ROOMS AND RATES
The treehouse is from £125
a night per couple including
breakfast, with a weekend
minimum of a two-night stay.

SITUATED WITHIN THE grounds of "Coates Castle", a Strawberry Hill Gothic mansion, owners Alison and Ron have created three unique rooms in a treehouse, barn and country cottage. Their guests agree that a warm welcome and relaxing stay is guaranteed in this site surrounded by pretty gardens and woodland. The treehouse is built into a huge sweet chestnut tree on the edge of a wood, and a substantial staircase leads upstairs. There is a thatched room with a double bed set between the tree branches, looking out through large glass doors to the treetops. The room has an en suite shower with a glass roof and is covered with handmade mosaic tiles. A large balcony with swing seats is an added touch for lazily reading the Sunday papers or evening drinks.

There is also a double room in the nearby cottage as well as in the barn, whose bedroom is reached by a spiral staircase. All rooms have double beds with fine cotton sheets, tea and coffee-making facilities with homemade biscuits, TV and a hairdryer. The en suite bath/shower rooms have soft fluffy towels and handmade soaps.

While the treehouse is particularly recommended, memorable breakfasts are served for all guests, using organic free-range eggs and quality sausages and bacon. They are served in the heated conservatory or outside the walled garden during the summer.

GUEST COMMENTS

• *A unique experience, both fun and romantic.*
• *Everything just wonderful — thank you for the dream "Africa in Sussex".*
• *A beautiful love nest in a tree — just made to set your spirit free.*
• *"Quality"!! Paradise in the tree tops! Thank you, thank you and thank you again, for such a magical stay. Your hospitality was second to none. An enchanted tree house in an enchanted wood. Incredible.*

TO DO

Fittleworth is in the middle of fabulous walking and cycling country with paths leading from the front door. Numerous public rights of way and the 80 mile long South Downs Way are close by.

CRAZY BEAR HOTEL – BEACONSFIELD

Luxury design at its most dramatic

THE CRAZY BEAR ❷❽
Old Beaconsfield
Bucks HP9 1LX
01494 673086
enquiries@crazybear-
beaconsfield.co.uk
www.crazybeargroup.co.uk

ROOMS AND RATES
Ten suites from £200–£550.

LOCATION
Just off the M40 motorway,
about 30 minutes from
central London or Heathrow.

THE OLDEST DOCUMENTED building in Beaconsfield has been magnificently restored over four years in a made-to-order, without restraint, makeover. Its redesign can only be described as awesome – dramatic architecture, luxurious materials, spectacular lighting and even an underground extension create an elaborate, luxurious property.

Each of the ten individually designed bedrooms uses materials to dramatic effect. Textured leather, suede, oak, porcelain, velvet and lots of gold leaf decorate rooms which are themselves filled with statement furniture and theatrical ornamentation.

The main bar is a work of art in its own right. From an Italian jade marble floor and gloss-polished walnut and copper bar, to the two huge skylights where a row of six 1930s crystal chandeliers sit, all is top-to-toe luxury. Along one wall is a custom-made, 55 ft black Chesterfield, studded with Swarovski crystals. There are polished pewter tables and stools. Heavy crushed-velvet curtains drape from antique hand-carved oak panelling to complete the extreme decor.

A grand white marble staircase with an elaborate iron-work vine sculpture and python banister leads to the private bar, The Crystal Room. This underground Aladdin's cave has mirrored walls, ceiling and fibre-optic lighting effects, and is tastefully furnished with lots of pewter. Seating is white embossed leather with a matching black leather floor.

Fine dining is provided with an English restaurant featuring a huge open fire, crystal studded Chesterfield seating, textured leather and 24 carat gold leaf walls and polished antique oak flooring. The nearby Thai restaurant has embossed velvet walls, four huge crystal chandeliers hanging from the vaulted ceiling, leather tables and banquette seating.

A number of meeting and private room facilities are provided, including The Library, which as well as a giant wall bookcase has a 18 ft bird-walnut boardroom dining table, highly lacquered gold and black wall panelling, textured leather and more chandeliers.

The Hunting Lodge is full of rustic wood and taxidermy, including a huge Victorian moose head and antique antlers. The Thai Snug is made from reclaimed Gothic church panelling.

To complete the luxury of this property, the small garden has an infinity swimming pool and jacuzzi – kept at steaming-hot temperature throughout the year.

VISITOR COMMENT

"Uninhibited and uncompromised design – a masterpiece."

HAMPTON COURT PALACE

Grace and Favour apartments in historic royal palace

HAMPTON COURT PALACE 29
East Molesey, Surrey

THE LANDMARK TRUST
Shottesbrooke
Maidenhead
Berkshire SL6 3SW
01628 825925
bookings@landmarktrust.org.uk
www.landmarktrust.org.uk

ROOMS AND RATES
Fish Court has four
bedrooms and sleeps up
to six, while The Georgian
House accommodates up to
eight in a variety of single,
double and twin rooms.
Prices for each property
vary from £654 for a
four-night midweek break
in January to £2,874 for a
week in July / August.

HAMPTON COURT PLACE is no empty museum and The Landmark Trust has been granted the opportunity to allow members of the public to stay in two properties on behalf of custodians, Historic Royal Palaces. The tradition of loyal servants of the crown being allowed to remain in royal apartments after completion of service follows a precedent known as Grace and Favour that was set by George III.

The palace itself needs little introduction. Visitors staying here get a sense of a secret life beyond the public eye – of doors leading to invisible corridors, of figures disappearing up a staircase with a shopping basket, of a life beyond the security barriers in one of the most loved of Henry VIII's palaces.

Fish Court is an apartment in the serving wing of the Tudor Palace, originally provided for the Officers of the Pastry and adjoining the main palace. Famous for his lavish entertaining, Henry VIII commissioned many new kitchens including one entirely for the baking of pies.

The Georgian House used to be home to the Clerk of Works for the palace and was also originally a kitchen, built in 1719. It provides a private walled garden into which the morning sun shines and includes attic bedrooms that overlook the beautiful palace roofs.

VISITOR COMMENTS

• *We are sure that not even Hogwarts could seem more magical.*

• *We never dreamed we would be able to stay in Henry VIII's home. What a gracious host he was.*

TO DO

Guests are free to explore the gardens and most of the courtyards at all times, early and late, and the public rooms of the palace during opening hours. If you should ever tire of the amazing opportunities your access provides, London is only 35 minutes by train and the River Thames is alongside, offering boat trips to Kingston and Richmond.

PAVILION HOTEL

Rock'n'roll chic in this inspired art hotel

PAVILION HOTEL ③
34–36 Sussex Gardens
Hyde Park
London W2
0207 262 0905
info@pavilionhoteluk.com
www.pavilionhoteluk.com

ROOMS AND RATES
Thirty rooms. Single rooms
are from £60 to £85 and
doubles and twin rooms
£100. Family rooms are £130.
Prices are per room, per night
and inclusive of continental
breakfast and taxes.

LOCATION
The hotel is a 5 minute
walk from Edgware Road
underground station on
the Circle or District lines
and perhaps a 10 minute
taxi ride from mainline
stations. It is 20 minutes
on foot to Hyde Park and
the Oxford Street shops.

SOURCING FABRICS, WALLPAPER, room fixtures and fittings from around the world, Danny and his sister Noshi converted a once-neglected London townhouse hotel into an artistic and funky place to hang out. From minimalist decor in some rooms, to funky 70s, their thirty rooms cater for a variety of tastes. Rooms are eccentrically crammed with delicate artefacts that in some cases, have not stood up to the relentless wear of guests and souvenir hunters. Be prepared to go with the flow, and recognize that this property caters for a budget-conscious audience, keen to have a memorable experience and willing to forgo the frills of higher priced London properties. Although equipped with TV / DVD combos, don't expect the rooms to be large and be prepared for small but functional en suite facilities. The sizes and styles vary, from the tiny "Quiet Please" single room, to the opulence of "White Days Soul Nights". Everyone has their favourites – from those that you want to sleep in yourselves, such as the four-poster of "Indian Summer", to those that you just want to tell your friends about – such as the mirror beads and 70s disco fever glitter-ball look of Honky Tonk Afro.

Both Noshi and Danny are friendly hosts and they have built a great reputation with stars from the TV and music industry keen to sample somewhere with character at very affordable prices. Bryan Ferry, Duran Duran and other 80s heyday artists still call the Pavilion home when playing in London, as does regular guest Courtney Pine. Kate Moss and Pete Docherty were one-time regular guests, although Pete is now banned after hosting a particularly memorable niche gig, trashing his bedroom in the process.

A limited continental breakfast is left on a tray outside your room, although a "full English" is available in the dining room of the adjoining hotel for an additional charge if requested in advance.

TO DO

London needs no introduction, and the hotel is close to tube and mainline rail stations. There is a thriving Lebanese community on nearby Edgware Road, a few minutes' walk from the hotel. You'll find falafel restaurants and bars all the way down this busy street open most of the night.

HOTEL PELIROCCO

Funky themed hotel inspired by pop culture, sexy sirens and maverick musicians

HOTEL PELIROCCO **32**
10 Regency Square
Brighton BN1 2FG
01273 327055
info@hotelpelirocco.co.uk
www.hotelpelirocco.co.uk

ROOMS AND RATES
The hotel has a total of
nineteen rooms, singles
from £55 midweek rising
to £65 at weekends. Double
rooms are from £115–£145
at weekends inclusive of
a generous breakfast.

LOCATION
There is an underground NCP
car park opposite the hotel.
Hotel Pelirocco is within
walking distance of shops,
seafront and staggering
distance from Brighton's
club and restaurant scene.

AN UPDATED TOWNHOUSE bed and breakfast off Regency Square offering funky themed rooms inspired by pop culture, sexy sirens and maverick musicians. One of the first Brighton B&B hotels to add a little extra to guest experiences, Hotel Pelirocco gives you an opportunity to have fun. Some of the nineteen rooms on offer are in need of a lick of paint and a little TLC, but there are a number of great rooms that won't disappoint guests willing to put quirky style above a detailed designer finish. This is not an up-market boutique property with bespoke fittings – and your bathroom is unlikely to be a highlight. However the staff are friendly and want you to enjoy your stay, so if you're unhappy don't be afraid to speak out. If a different room is available, ask if they'll offer you the option to move.

Some of the rooms celebrate Brighton's saucier past, none more so than the "Play Room", which aims to be the hotels "dirty weekend" suite. Dedicated to all things decadent and indulgent, it combines kitsch and sexy boudoir with a circular bed and mirrored ceiling. Equally fun is the "Pin Up Parlour", styled after sex symbol Diana Dors. It's not all sex, however, and music lovers might be interested in the "Rough Trade Rough Nite" room, inspired by the original Rough Trade Record Shop in west London. A single-occupancy room, it has a record deck with headphones and record promos to play.

When staying in one of the top-floor rooms, the great news is that they've recently renovated the previously slow elevator. In the past it was regularly out of action and you had to negotiate a narrow staircase to your room.

TO DO

If you're interested, the "Play Room" has its own lap-dancing pole and you can book a lesson from a professional to learn the right moves. The hotel "playstation" bar is open until 4am on Friday and Saturday nights. Late-night Brighton needs little introduction and the hotel staff give recommendations for the best restaurants and nightclubs to suit every taste.

LIVINGSTONE SAFARI LODGE

Safari lodges viewing zebra and wildebeest on Romney Marsh

PORT LYMPNE WILD 34
ANIMAL PARK
Lympne
Nr Hythe
Kent CT21 4PD
01303 234190
info@howletts.net
www.totallywild.net

LOCATION AND RATES
Lympne is situated on the
sea cliffs above Romney
Marsh in Kent, some 7
miles west of Folkestone.
Off-peak prices of £150 per
person, based on two adults
sharing a luxury tent, they
include a drive around the
reserve with the rangers and
breakfast. Single occupancy
is £250. There are reductions
for children aged 9–14.
Children under 9 are not
admitted to the safari lodges.

THE 600 ACRE Port Lympne Wild Animal Park is world re-nowned for its endangered species breeding programmes. The park now offers a 100 acre African safari experience, with tented lodge accommodation in the reserve itself, al-lowing guests to see giraffes and zebras roaming the park as well as the chance of glimpsing the gorillas, leopards and elephants among its 300 animals.

Obviously health and safety restrictions prohibit an exact replica of the Serengeti, and your view is of the Kentish coast rather than Kilimanjaro. However, the animals are certainly real enough, as the reserve is home to the larg-est breeding herd of black rhinos outside Africa, as well as Siberian and Indian tigers, African elephants, Barbary lions and many other rare and endangered species. The tents are like those found on a luxury safari, as are the knowledgea-ble rangers. Over sundowners on the veranda you'll learn of their conservation activities and hear "experiences and sto-ries from the bush" during your African dinner. You'll then retire to sleep in a "proper" bed, to wake up early with the calls of the animals, ready for a dawn tour. The vista is stun-ning, with views across to France on a clear day. Giraffes lope past your viewing platform, and the wildebeest graze by the watering hole.

You can sleep soundly in the knowledge that your visit will help to fund conservation work while giving you a taste of the African safari, with the chance to be back at work by lunchtime.

TO DO

Staying at the lodge is intended as a fun experience, but there is a real conservation message. The park and the Aspinall Foundation that it supports were set up by the late John Aspinall, with the aim of protecting and breeding rare and endangered species and returning them to safe areas in their native homeland.

SUGGESTIONS TO CHECK OUT
WHEN YOU CHECK IN

Sea Spray Hotel, see opposite page

XORON FLOATING HOTEL ㉑

Paul and Wendy were the originators of the often copied term "floatel", for their converted 1941 naval gunboat bed and breakfast. Friendly hosts, they can recommend the best pubs locally to visit for lunch or evening drinks.
• Five en suite cabins from £28 per person per night. • **Embankment Road** Bembridge, Isle of Wight PO35 5NS
• 01983 874596 • www.xoronfloatel.co.uk

ISLAND CHARTERS B&B ㉒

Floating boats
These floating B&B boats are moored in Wootton Creek. Guests stay in either the 98 ft MV Newclose barge, or MV Sea Wasp, a 65 ft cruiser. The boats have a mixture of en suite cabins with access to a communal lounge and sundeck.
• £44–£50, single £22–£25.
• **Sea Urchin,** 26 Barge Lane, Wootton, Isle of Wight PO33 4LB • 01983 882315
• www.island-charters-bandb.co.uk

MALMAISON ㉔

The former local Oxford prison
The local Oxford prison, converted to more luxurious accommodation, by the Malmaison chain of up-market hotels.
• From £180 per night for a double room and from £245 per night for a suite.
• 3 Oxford Castle, Oxford, Oxon OX1 1AY • 01865 268400
• oxford@malmaison.com
• www.malmaison-oxford.com

MILLER'S RESIDENCE ㉚

This eight-bedroom property is luxuriously furnished in the style of the 18th century, and centrally located in chic Notting Hill. Rooms are named after English romantic poets, and filled with antiques, bric-a-brac and ornaments as befits the owner, antique expert Martin Miller – a most gregarious and jovial host.
• Doubles from £177–£270, inclusive of evening cocktails and breakfast.
• **111a Westbourne Grove**, London W2 4UW • 0207 243 1024
• www.millersuk.com

SEA SPRAY HOTEL ㉝

In keeping with Brighton's reputation as a saucy get-away, this hotel offers a number of themed suites including the Las Vegas kitsch of the Elvis bedroom, and the feather boas and crushed red velvet of the Boudoir. If you're driving, ask if they have any resident parking vouchers available, which are considerably cheaper than meter parking.
• Thirteen rooms with weekend rates for the Elvis room from £135 and for the Boudoir from £199 per room, inclusive of breakfast. Check with the hotel for restrictions and midweek special offers.
• **Sea Spray Hotel,** 26 New Steine, Brighton BN2 1PD • 01273 680332
• www.seaspraybrighton.co.uk

LODESMAN AND KHINA LIGHTHOUSE COTTAGES ㉟

Located in an acre of lawned grounds around North Foreland Lighthouse, on the chalk headland above the seaside town of Broadstairs in Kent, the cottages are child-friendly, set well away from the cliffs and only 3 minutes from the sandy beach at Joss Bay. Bookings are managed by Rural Retreats on behalf of Trinity House, who offer two guest cottages, sleeping four apiece on a self-catering basis.
• The minimum booking for four guests in either of the cottages in low winter season is two nights with pricing from £263 per property. In high summer the minimum is seven nights and pricing is from £963.
• **Rural Retreats,** Draycott Business Park, Draycott, Moreton-in-Marsh, Gloucestershire GL56 9JY • 01386 701177
• www.ruralretreats.co.uk

WALES
& WEST MIDLANDS

CABAN CASITA

Groovy cabin with dedicated dog room

CABAN CASITA 36
Cenarth Waterfalls,
West Wales

UNDER THE THATCH
Bryn Hawen
Henllan
Llandysul
Ceredigion SA44 5UA
01239 851 410
post@underthethatch.co.uk
www.underthethatch.co.uk

ROOMS AND RATES
Two-night low-season
breaks (March) from £138,
plus £12 / £18 for dog(s).
A week in high season
(August) is £528.

LOCATION
Situated in Penlan woodland
holiday village in Cenarth
on the border between
Carmarthenshire and
Pembrokeshire. This is a
very quiet, quality holiday
village of privately owned
cabins carefully landscaped
into acres of woods.
While you can see other
cabins from Caban Casita,
they are arranged around
woodland cul-de-sacs and
aren't close enough to make
you feel overlooked.

CABAN CASITA IS sister cabin to Caban Cariad, "The Loveshack", which won the 2007 Top 5 UK Log Cabins award. Clad in pine along Scandinavian lines in a woodland setting, genuine designer pieces have been mixed with modern conveniences and a contemporary pebble fire to celebrate the best in 1960s and 1970s design. Check out the fabulous Eero Aarnio globe chair which is Dr Greg Stevenson's pride and joy! It is 1970s groovy, not 1970s grim!

The cabin has two bedrooms – one cosy double, and the second (originally a bunkroom) has been converted specifically for dogs. Fed up of trying to find nice places to take his dog Minti on holiday, Greg designed this cabin to be dog-friendly – with wipe-clean pine floors, washable pet bedding, etc. The room has a fitted dog-bed with feeding and water bowls provided, and ventilation to the woods outside. Please bring your pet's favourite blankets.

The compact galley kitchen is adequate with full-size appliances. Groovy tableware adds a nice retro touch. The toilet / shower room is clean and functional. There are more facilities on site, including a heated swimming pool during the summer.

TO DO

Perfect for just lounging about, there is plenty to do on site. Facilities are seasonal, but include a heated outdoor pool, sauna, solarium, and bar with home cinema. Just outside your cabin door are marked forest footpaths and any time of the year there will be a pub serving good food, and a shop selling the essentials, within walking distance of the cabin.

VISITOR COMMENTS

• *Dog heaven!*
• *A fantastic break – just what the doctor ordered!*

WENDY – THE ABERPORTH EXPRESS

"Beached" Edwardian rail carriage on Heritage Coast

WENDY ❸❼
THE ABERPORTH EXPRESS
Aberporth, West Wales

ROOMS AND RATES
Low season (May) two-night breaks from £146. Seven nights in peak season (August) at £615. Pembrokeshire is only a 25 minute drive, however there is no vehicular access to the property itself. Access from the car park is via a 300 yard level gravel footpath. Prices include hot water, electricity, heating and the first basket of wood/coal for the fire/stove.

UNDER THE THATCH
Bryn Hawen
Henllan
Llandysul
Ceredigion SA44 5UA
01239 851 410
post@underthethatch.co.uk
www.underthethatch.co.uk

THIS FORMER GREAT Western Railway sleeping carriage has been relocated alongside a footpath in Wales with panoramic views of the Ceredigion Heritage Coast. Called Wendy after the character in Peter Pan, which was published the year before the carriage was built in 1905, it travelled the length and breadth of the Great Western line between England and Wales until it was retired in 1937.

Permission to build a permanent structure in this location would never be granted, so the opportunity to stay in something with its own history while you enjoy the view is particularly pleasing.

There are two insulated and oak-lined double bedrooms with proper sprung mattresses and a single children's bed, allowing you to sleep in comfort all year round. A modern kitchen and bathroom complete the rental package.

There is a lounge and dining compartment with a period 1930s dining table. Every room has uninterrupted country and/or sea views with open fields to the rear, sea to the front. This is a peaceful location with no roads within 300 yards, and no neighbours or noise pollution.

The location is idyllic and your needs are catered for by a village pub, shop and food within a 5 minute walk – which includes a Chinese take-away and beachside café if you can't bear to cook.

VISITOR COMMENTS

- *Wendy is fantastic – What a location!*
- *Every day we walked to a different beach.*
- *A BRILLIANT holiday – weather great, views spectacular, dolphins & seals seen. Lots to explore lovely beaches, and great food ... we'll be back!*

BLACK MOUNTAIN YURT

Camping for those who don't do camping

BLACK MOUNTAIN YURT ❹
Brecon Beacons
National Park, Wales

UNDER THE THATCH
Bryn Hawen
Henllan
Llandysul
Ceredigion SA44 5UA
01239 851 410
post@underthethatch.co.uk
www.underthethatch.co.uk

ROOMS AND RATES
Low season (May) two-
night breaks from £138.
High season (August)
weeks at £505.
The yurt is in a field about
50 yards' walk from the end
of a short private lane, out
of sight of the converted
stables and farm buildings.
The location is on the slope
of the Black Mountain on the
western side of the Brecon
Beacons National Park, not
to be confused with the
Black Mountains to the east.

THOSE WARY OF camping for fear of getting cold, or lacking a more substantial bed, have never slept in a yurt. Snug, with felt insulation and proper flooring, you still get a fantastic outdoor vibe from living in the landscape, but can retreat to your creature comforts.

Yurts are camping for those who don't do camping!

Black Mountain Yurt is a Mongolian original of good quality, with furnishings hand painted in traditional designs. There is a wood-burning stove, sofa and dining table and double/twin beds. Bathroom facilities are a worry for many, and stepping up from tradition, you are provided with a converted shepherd's wagon with power shower, gas combi-boiler and a camping luxury – a flush toilet. The shepherd's wagon also provides the small kitchen with fridge, gas cooker, oven and grill. There's even a microwave.

There's plenty of space inside the 16 ft diameter yurt for two, in great comfort. With a seating area outside, you can enjoy your own peaceful meadow with lovely views of the National Park and secluded woodland all around.

TO DO

The yurt has a peaceful setting in the National Park and there are many activities within walking or (short) driving distance, including visits to many local castles. Check out Llandeilo, a mile away. Named the most chic place in Wales, it is not only a charming and very pretty town, but also a gourmet destination with three delicatessens for picnic supplies.

VISITOR COMMENTS

• *It was hard to drag ourselves away from the yurt to experience the beautiful landscape and coastline.*

• *One week wasn't enough! So much to see and do in this beautiful place.*

SNOWDONIA MANOR – PLAS Y DDUALLT

Historic house accessed by private platform of mountain railway

PLAS Y DDUALLT ❹❸
Tan y Bwlch
Blaenau Ffestiniog
Gwynedd LL41 3YT
01766 590272
enquiries@
snowdoniamanor.co.uk
www.snowdoniamanor.co.uk

ROOMS AND RATES
The manor house is available as a film location and the adjoining cottage can be rented on a self-catering basis. The cottage has two bedrooms, sleeping four people in total, and has a secluded garden with five cascading ponds. The cottage costs from £360 to £550 per week. Prices are inclusive of linen, towels and electricity as well as central heating when necessary, but excluding the weekly rover tickets for the railway. In 2008 these are available at £17.50 per adult per week – fantastic value!

PLAS Y DDUALLT, literally the «house on the black hillside», is steeped in history and folklore. Set high up in Snowdonia National Park, this Grade II listed building borders the Ffestiniog Mountain Railway and the Maentwrog Nature Reserve. It is one of the oldest inhabited houses in Wales, dating back to the 15th century, and access until the 1960s was either on foot or by train. Now, guests can use a steep tarmac drive that winds its way for half a mile, climbing 500 ft through ancient woodlands, although old habits die slowly and train access is preferred.

Colonel Campbell restored and renovated the property in the 1960s. The colonel was quite a character and a great friend of the railway. He used his explosives expertise to help blast the new route for the Ffestiniog Mountain Railway, which runs above the house, about a minute's walk from the front door. From March until October there are quite a few trains each day. On a busy day in August there are eight trains up the line and eight trains down. Guests stick out their hand from Campbell's platform, their own private halt, and a steam train will grind to a halt.

The platform provides a great vantage point from which to appreciate trains coming up the line. You can hear the distant whistle as they pull away from Tan y Bwlch station and, as they approach, the plumes of steam puff out above the trees. Finally the train emerges round a bend, a panorama of a dozen carriages chugging their way up the hillside.

TO DO

Tucked away in 160 acres of ancient woodland, the property is secluded and peaceful apart from the occasional cry of a buzzard and the bleating of sheep. A walk from the back door up Moelwyn Mawr and along the ridge over Craigysgafn and Moelwyn Bach offers breathtaking views of the coastline and Snowdonia. This and other circular routes can be comfortably achieved within a day. Worth a visit is the Italian-style village of Portmerion, created by local architect Sir Clough Williams-Ellis, a short journey down the line from Campbell's platform. A detailed timetable is available from the Ffestiniog Railway website.

THE LIGHTHOUSE

Lighthouse fortress, on cliff edge with amazing views

MARINE DRIVE 🔴
Great Orme's Head
Llandudno
Conwy LL30 2XD
01492 876819
enquiries@lighthouse-
llandudno.co.uk
www.lighthouse-
llandudno.co.uk

ROOMS AND RATES
All three suites are £75 per person per night, with £20 supplement for singles.

LOCATION
The Lighthouse is situated off the Great Orme Scenic Route (Marine Drive), some 2 miles from the Toll Gate Cottage.

THIS IMMENSELY SOLID lighthouse was built in 1862, using dressed limestone and vast bulks of Canadian pitch pine, to resemble a castle. The panoramic view from The Lamp Room through some 200° east to west is especially impressive. The beacon remained in continuous use until 1985, when the optic was removed to the visitor centre on the summit of Great Orme.

Three rooms are available. The Principal Keeper's Suite, with its four-poster bed, en suite shower and easterly sea view. The Telegraph Room, which is a double room with sea views to north and east. It has original telescope apertures in the pine shutters and a cosy sitting area with a traditional black slate fireplace. Finally, The Lamp Room, also a double, has floor-to-ceiling windows through which the beacon once shone. If sea views are something you enjoy, you cannot fail to be enthralled.

Worth special mention is breakfast, taken in the north-facing Victorian dining room, which allows guests to look down over a 360 ft vertical drop while enjoying a traditional Welsh breakfast.

TO DO

The Lighthouse is within the Great Orme Country Park, providing a peaceful setting to enjoy the magnificent scenery and wildlife. Near the seaside resort of Llandudno there are numerous pubs and restaurants, the North Wales Theatre, and some of the best shopping facilities in North Wales. As a major tourist destination, there are facilities for golf, tennis, sea or freshwater fishing and pony trekking within a few miles. Medieval Conwy, a World Heritage centre, is only 7 miles away and guests can visit its famous castle, Plas Mawr (a lovingly restored Elizabethan townhouse), and also walk the town's ancient walls.

SHOWMAN'S WAGGON

Posh camping in circus ringmaster's waggon

SHOWMAN'S WAGGON 46
"Welsh Lake District", Wales

UNDER THE THATCH
Bryn Hawen
Henllan
Llandysul
Ceredigion SA44 5UA
01239 851 410
post@underthethatch.co.uk
www.underthethatch.co.uk
West Usk Lighthouse

ROOMS AND RATES
Two-night low-season breaks
(e.g. January) from £127.
A week in peak season
(August) is £533.
For two people, set in 1½
acres of private meadow
with direct access to open
moorland for walking, you
have 1½ miles of private
river frontage to explore.
There is a genuine
sense of being close to
nature and wildlife.

STAY IN A restored 1940s Showman's Waggon and escape to the beautiful Wye Valley in mid Wales. This riverside location is a chance to get close to nature in a secluded spot, with modern conveniences and the luxury of a proper bed and wood-burning stove.

Built in the 1940s, the waggon would have been the "living van" home of a travelling showman from a circus – like a grand form of early caravan with its own kitchen, living room and bedroom. The interior is fantastic – all wood-lined with cut-glass mirrors, old lamps, a wood-burning stove, bureau and leather tub chairs.

Following restoration, Under the Thatch is able to let it for holidays in its own woodland location with wonderful open views and a great sense of seclusion.

The accommodation offers a compact kitchen with full-size gas cooker, fridge and sink plus a lounge. The double bed is 6'4 inches long but narrower than a modern standard double, a cosy nest for two. Views down the valley make getting out of bed seem worthwhile.

Alongside is a hay barn for the exclusive use of guests, with a small heated shower room and toilet. The main farmhouse is a field away, offering a games room where you can play table-tennis, table-football and pool.

VISITOR COMMENTS
• *What an absolutely idyllic "old-world" retreat from the modern hustle and bustle of everyday life – the place is amazing.*
• *The waggon is beautiful, and I loved waking up to such stunning views every morning.*

CLEDAN VALLEY TIPIS

Hill farm location for tipis

4 BANK HOUSE 🔑
Carno
Caersws
Powys SY17 5LR
01686 420409
tipis@cledanvalleytipi.co.uk
www.cledanvalleytipi.co.uk

ROOMS AND RATES
The site is down a quiet country lane in the village of Carno, between the market towns of Llanidloes, Newtown and Machynlleth. Open between Easter and September. A single night for two is £75, while seven nights cost £350. The 21 ft tipis for four cost between £90 for a single night to £450 for a week. Outside peak season, midweek special discounts apply.

FROM A HONEYMOON suite for two that nestles amongst a stand of native trees next to a stream, to larger family tipis for up to six guests, this 7 acre site only has eight tipis, so everyone gets a little seclusion. As well as family tipis, there are two others for couples, located within earshot of the calming sound of the upland stream that gives Cledan Valley its name.

Putting family tipis close to the facilities, away from the river, and the romantic tipis away from the main field and close to the river, the Cledan Valley team aim to find the appropriate location for your needs. They will shortly provide a tipi location suitable for disabled guests with wheelchair access too. Family tipis are 21 ft or 22 ft in diameter and sleep four or six people comfortably. The 21 ft tipi comes with one double futon bed and four singles, and the 22 ft comes with two double futons and two singles. If it's early or late season you might wish to use the supplied fire bowl or fire basket, but if you've got young children or feel uncomfortable with the fire inside, you can make a fire outside and have a little extra space.

Their flagship "Main Lodge" tipi easily sleeps eight people; this is ideal for when you have a big group or indeed just want the extra space. The more secluded pitches, almost out of sight of the rest of the field, have a climb to get to the shower block or car park, but this is more than compensated for by their locations that make you really feel like you're in a world of your own.

All tipis come with a double futon bed, sheepskin rugs, open hearth fire and firewood, a trivet to cook on, plus a gas cooker, cool box with a daily chiller refill, blanket box, cutlery, plates, glasses and cups. There is a charcoal barbeque, picnic bench and table outside each tipi as well. All you need to bring is your duvet or sleeping bag, and a little food or drink – although the local Spar shop is open seven days a week until 8 pm and provides most staples.

WEST USK LIGHTHOUSE

Lighthouse on River Severn estuary

ST BRIDES WENTLOOG ⑱
Newport
Gwent, NP10 8SF
01633 810126
info@westusklighthouse.co.uk
www.westusklighthouse.co.uk

ROOMS AND RATES
Situated between Newport
and Cardiff at the end
of a rocky private road,
the lighthouse is now a
Grade II listed building.
Bed and breakfast room
rate in the lighthouse, for
two people, is £110–£150
per night. Single rooms are
from £75–£110 per night.
Special weekday rates
are sometimes offered
on late availability.

A FEW MILES from Newport, this accessible lighthouse at the junction of the Severn and Usk estuaries has views far out into the Bristol Channel. Built in 1821 on an island where the Severn and Usk run into the sea, it has a unique design. Not tall like most lighthouses, and considerably bigger in circumference, all accommodation is within the building itself. Rooms are wedge-shaped and the stone spiral staircase in the centre is found above a collecting well. In 1922 the lighthouse was decommissioned and for a short while it became a private house but soon fell into disrepair. Some of the surrounding sea was reclaimed and the island became connected to the mainland.

The current owners bought it in 1987 and, following a two-year restoration project to make it habitable once again, have turned it into a quirky bed and breakfast property that guests can enjoy today. On one side the sea is the loudest sound, especially when the tide (the second fastest in the world) comes racing in to the foot of the building, while on the other side you only hear the occasional mooing cow. The view is fantastic and the winter sunsets amazing.

In addition to the lighthouse, the owners have recently installed a 21 ft Mongolian yurt, available on a B&B basis or as a conference and meeting space.

TO DO

The lighthouse is a great place where guests can chill out and relax if they want to, either as a romantic getaway or for an indulgent hen night or family reunion.

There are ten golf courses locally and the nearby Celtic Manor hotel, just outside Newport, plays host to the Ryder Cup 2010. Partners who are not into golf can be pampered with the many complementary therapies on offer at the lighthouse itself, such as aromatherapy, reflexology, Indian head massage and reiki, by prior arrangement. There is also a waterbed with a built in massager!

On the Welsh side of the Severn crossing there is plenty to do, without having to pay the toll to cross the Severn to Bristol. Nearby are the castles of Chepstow, Caldicot and the Roman city of Caerleon. Of particular interest is Tredegar House, with its lake and craft shops in the grounds, as well as the romantic little Castell Coch ("Red Castle").

Newport has an amazing "transporter" bridge that carries cars in a hanging gondola 242 ft above the roadway across the River Usk. Currently undergoing renovation, it is worth a visit when it reopens. Cardiff is 25 minutes by car, with the Welsh National Museum, Millennium Stadium and Techniquest museums open all year round.

CAPEL PENTWYN

Converted chapel with views over the Wye Valley and Forest of Dean

Ty'r Wennol ⑭
Croes Faen
Penallt
Monmouthshire NP25 4SB
01600 71 781
qwest@btconnect.com
www.capelpentwyn.co.uk

Rooms and rates
Three-night packages from £300 in low season rising to £400 in high season. Seven-night stays are from £500 in low season, rising to £700 in high season. Extra charges for pets apply, however there are discounts of 25% for couples.

St Mary's church was built in 1869 at the height of the Arts and Crafts period. Capel Pentwyn is a 2005 conversion of the church, which was deconsecrated in 2003. It adjoins the Old School, which is also available to rent. Sleeping up to five, it has been sensitively converted by local architects to reflect the style of the late Victorian period. Externally, little has been changed except for a simple garden, parking for three cars and a large terrace giving panoramic views over the valley and to the nearby Forest of Dean. Internally, it has been sensitively converted to comfortable accommodation. An entrance lobby soars to the rafters and a gallery from the first floor overlooks the entrance. The apse, with wonderful stained-glass windows, forms an elegant dining room with the original Victorian tiles reset in an oak floor that covers the whole ground area. The large lounge has oriental rugs and period tapestries and an antique wood-burning stove of the period imported from Norway, resting on a hearth created by a local sculptor from Forest of Dean stone.

The building has been designed with attention to the needs of those who may have disabilities and there is a downstairs single study bedroom and a "wheel-in" shower and bathroom. The whole ground floor and garden is wheelchair friendly.

TO DO
Capel Pentwyn adjoins the Old School, which has also been restored, and together the two can accommodate eleven people for larger groups, a house party or a special occasion.

THE CITADEL

Pink castle built for mother and sister in the 1820s

Weston-under-Redcastle
Near Shrewsbury
Shropshire SY4 5JY
01630 685 204
griffiths@
thecitadelweston.co.uk
www.thecitadelweston.co.uk

ROOMS AND RATES
There are three guest suites.
The West Bedroom provides
a double bed, sitting room
and bathroom, and is
£48–£60 per person.
The Round Room is a
double / twin with en
suite bathroom and priced
at £48–£60 per person.
Finally, the Hill Room is
another double / twin with
en suite shower room, at
£45–£55 per person
Dinner by prior arrangement
(not Sunday) is £28. As
the owners do not have an
alcohol licence, guests are
welcome to bring their own
wine. A number of local
pubs offer good food, with
recommendations offered.

CONSTRUCTED IN LOCAL salmon-red sandstone, the citadel was built by Sir Rowland Hill for his mother and sister Jane in the 1820s. Ingeniously designed in the form of three inter-linked towers set to the points of a triangle, round every bend is something to catch the eye – a Victorian grotto, a shady glade full of acers or even a walled potager.

The Griffiths family has lived at the Citadel since 1957, and current owners Sylvia and husband Beverley own the farm, some 200 acres, which surrounds the property.

There are three guest bedrooms in the north and west towers. Two have separate bathrooms and the third has en suite shower and toilet facilities. All have clear views of the North Shropshire countryside.

Guests have use of the west lounge, which adjoins the billiard room, with a full-size table available. They experience a house-party atmosphere, eating and chatting around the large Regency table in a dining room with a ceiling embossed with vines.

The 3 acre garden, laid partly to lawn, lies to the south and west of the house. At its core is a sandstone rocky outcrop with paths that wind right round and over it. On the far side of the garden is a thatched Victorian-style summerhouse. From there you can look across the kitchen garden, which provides nearly all the vegetables and soft fruit for the house and has the protection of a high Victorian brick wall. This part of the garden is formal in design, with interconnecting paved paths, and is as much ornamental as functional. It could be more accurately described as a potager – where vegetables and flowers happily intermingle.

TO DO

The property stands in a spectacular position in Hawkstone Park, looking out over farmland, the nearby golf course and the wooded escarpment of the Hawkstone hills.

THE SUMMERHOUSE

Elizabethan banqueting tower likened to fairytale castle

THE SUMMERHOUSE **51**
Eyton-on-Severn, Shropshire

THE VIVAT TRUST
70 Cowcross Street
London EC1M 6EJ
0207 336 8825
enquiries@vivat.org.uk
www.vivat.org.uk

ROOMS AND RATES
There is a single bed/sitting
room with a four-poster
bed and an open fireplace,
providing an intimate and
relaxed atmosphere.
Prices for a three-night
break start from £275.

LOCATION
Located in the tiny hamlet
of Eyton-on-Severn and
approached via a short length
of unmade estate road, the
property is 14 miles east of
Shrewsbury off the A458.

A RARE SURVIVING example of an Elizabethan banqueting tower, and originally one of a pair flanking the bowling green of Sir Francis Newport's family home at Eyton Hall.

Built on large estates a short distance from the main house, banqueting towers became popular in the late 16th century. Family members and guests retired to these intimate surroundings to savour the panoramic views and the heady scents and flavours of spiced wines, sweetmeats and the decorative sugar moulds of a banquet. The Summerhouse's likeness to a sugar-plum fairytale castle is intentional, as the intricate architecture was meant to reflect the elaborate dishes served.

The building has been restored by The Vivat Trust, which manages self-catering bookings for guests. It comprises two octagons, the larger of which provides the living space on two floors, and the smaller houses the oak staircase connecting the floors up to the balustraded roof terrace, offering outstanding views of the Shropshire countryside.

The kitchen is on the ground floor with fine views through three full-length arched windows. A toilet and shower room is enclosed underneath the stairs. The first floor provides a four-poster bedroom.

TO DO

Those who enjoy fine dining will perhaps already be familiar with the nearby Ludlow Food and Drink Festival and the area's reputation for great ingredients and restaurants. Ironbridge, Much Wenlock and Shrewsbury are all towns of historical note and worthy of day visits, as too are the National Trust properties of Attingham Park and Wilderthorpe Manor.

SUGGESTIONS TO CHECK OUT
WHEN YOU CHECK IN

The Summerhouse, see p.118

GYPSY CARAVAN AND CABIN ㊳

This authentic Gypsy caravan near Llangrannog, West Wales, is set in its own acre of riverside meadow and has the highest level of customer satisfaction of all Under the Thatch properties. In a wonderful rural location just a short drive from fantastic sandy beaches, you live close to nature. Comforts aren't however ignored and you also rent a small country cabin with a kitchen and shower-room for a unique holiday experience.
• **Under The Thatch,** Bryn Hawen, Henllan, Llandysul, Ceredigion SA44 5UA • 01239 851 410
• www.underthethatch.co.uk

NORTH STACK ㊴

An 1850s fog signal station
The redundant 1850s fog signal station has two bedrooms and is located in the Holyhead RSPB nature reserve, reached from the warden's house in owner Philippa Jacobs 4X4.
• Double room £70, single £40. • **Holyhead Mountain,** Holyhead, Isle of Anglesey LL65 IDU
• 01407 761252 • philippa.jacobs@hotmail.co.uk

THE MIRADOR GUEST HOUSE ㊶

Each of the six rooms at The Mirador has been themed according to Roman, Mediterranean, African, Spanish, Egyptian and Oriental styles, based on the travels of owners Philip and Jeanette Henry-Dean.
• Double rooms £79, single £59.
• **14 Mirador Crescent,** Swansea SA2 0QX
• 01792 466976 • www.themirador.co.uk

PORTMEIRION ㊷

Sleep in The Prisoner village
This Italianate village, made famous by the 1960s TV series, The Prisoner, offers rooms, suites and some quirky self-catering cottages, sleeping from three to eight people, including three for dog owners, within Portmeirion village itself.
• From £260 for the smallest cottage, low season. Hotel rooms per night from £170 for two, including breakfast. • **Portmeirion,** Gwynedd LL48 6ER
• 01766 770000 • www.portmeirion-village.com

ST CURIG'S CHURCH ㊹

A 19th-century church B&B
There are six bedrooms in this 19th-century church bed and breakfast. Although two of the rooms have four-poster beds and an outdoor hot tub is available, St Curig's (Capel Curig) has retained ecclesiastical features including stained-glass windows, a mosaic ceiling and a pulpit in one of the rooms.
• Double room £70–£75.
• **Capel Curig,** Gwynedd LL24 0EL
• 01690 720469 • www.stcurigschurch.com

THE LIBRARY HOUSE ㊾

This listed Georgian townhouse has three bedrooms and used to be the village library. It still has some of the original shelves, now filled with books and DVDs for guest use.
• Doubles £75–£100, singles £65–£75. • **Severn Bank,** Iron Bridge, Near Telford, Shropshire TF8 7AN • 01952 432299 • www.libraryhouse.com

THE TEMPLE ㊿

This classical folly dates from 1783 and was built as an architectural ornament from which to admire spectacular views. It is set within Badger Dingle, a 40 acre landscape of deep chasms and wooded ravines about 8 miles from Bridgnorth. With a double bedroom, the property is available on a self-catering basis from The Vivat Trust.
• Prices for a three-night break start from £275.
• **The Vivat Trust** • 0207 336 8825
• www.vivat.org.uk

ARLEY TOWER ⑭

This listed folly dates from 1842 and boasts a two-storey tower with a crenellated parapet and three-storey octagonal stair turret, complete with slit windows. It was originally built by a vengeful Earl Mountnorris to block the view from nearby Hafren House to the Upper Arley, an idyllic village nestling on the banks of the River Severn.
With a double bedroom, the property is available on a self-catering basis from The Vivat Trust.
• **The Vivat Trust** • 0207 336 8825
• www.vivat.org.uk

EAST MIDLANDS
& EAST ANGLIA

OSBASTON HOUSE

Goat herding on a Feather Down Farm

OSBASTON HOUSE **55**

ONLINE OR PHONE
BOOKING ONLY
01420 80804
info@featherdown.co.uk
www.featherdown.co.uk

ROOMS AND RATES
Each Feather Down Farm
tent can sleep up to five
adults (or up to six with
children) in a mixture of
double, bunk and a small
"cupboard" bed that is a real
hit with smaller children.
Most farm locations have
five tents. You can book for
weekends (Friday–Monday)
or midweek (Monday–Friday)
or for full weeks.
2009 prices start at £225 for
a midweek break. Required
linen packages are an
additional £5.95 per person.

LOCATION
Osbaston House Farm is
on the edge of 200 square
miles of The National Forest.
Two miles from the farm,
along pretty country lanes,
lies the vibrant market
town of Market Bosworth
which is surrounded by
many of Leicestershire's
pretty villages. Located 8
miles off the M1, Osbaston
House Farm is 90 minutes
from London and not
more than an hour from
Birmingham or Nottingham.

THE FEATHER DOWN Farm format of holidays in a working farm setting and rooms in a well-appointed luxury tent with modern conveniences has proved a hit in the UK and elsewhere. Established by one of the founders of Center Parcs, Feather Down Farms offer twenty-two locations in the UK as well as in Belgium, France and the Netherlands.

All locations offer similar accommodation, based around a huge tent with a raised wooden floor, open-plan dining table and wood-fired stove. Without electricity, the stove provides both cooking and heating. There is a cool box for refrigeration, with iced water bottles replenished daily. Evenings are candle or oil lantern lit, although you'll probably go to bed early to compensate for the early start that fresh air encourages. The (real) beds are comfortable with duvets provided and, most crucial of all for those more wary of camping, every tent has an adjoining flush toilet. Washing up is done the "old-fashioned" way, with water boiled from the kettle, and after a few hours to acclimatize, you'll start to appreciate the benefits of a more relaxed, rural pace of life. Tent kitchens are well equipped with pre-order cooking packages and towel hire additionally available. Apart from clothes and wellies, you don't really need to pack very much as the farm shop provides all the essentials, including locally sourced produce to eat.

TO DO

Of the many Feather Down Farm properties in the UK, 160 acre Osbaston House farm deserves special mention, because as well as small herds of cattle and sheep, they have diversified to become one of a handful of specialist goat farmers in the UK. These affectionate and intelligent animals are very child friendly and feeding time is a real opportunity for younger guests to get involved with day-to-day activities on a working farm. Osbaston House farm milks approximately 600 goats early in the morning and mid afternoon. Assistant shepherds and helpers are always welcome on a busy goat farm!

If you've ever wanted to be closer to nature, then the Feather Down Farm lifestyle will give you a break from TV. For anyone worried that there won't be enough to do, as well as bike hire at every location, each tent provides a cupboard stocked with family favourite board games. In addition, the farms themselves offer everyone the opportunity to enjoy the countryside and animals in a farm paddock, help bake bread in the wood oven and collect eggs from the chicken coop on every farm. You couldn't get a much fresher breakfast, or much closer to nature.

GOTHIC TEMPLE

Temple folly in the manicured landscape gardens of Stowe

GOTHIC TEMPLE **57**
Stowe, Buckinghamshire

THE LANDMARK TRUST
Shottesbrooke
Maidenhead
Berkshire SL6 3SW
01628 825925
bookings@landmarktrust.org.uk
www.landmarktrust.org.uk

ROOMS AND RATES
The temple can accommodate
up to four guests in two
double bedrooms. Prices
for the whole property are
from £342 for a four-night
midweek break in January
to £1,541 for a week in
July / August. Disabled
access is limited because
of the spiral staircase.

LOCATION
Between Oxford and
Northampton, Stowe's
nearest major town is
Buckingham – which has all
the trappings of a successful
market town with shops,
pubs and restaurants.

STOWE SCHOOL OFFERED The Landmark Trust a long lease on this property in 1970, whose efforts provide income to maintain this splendid example of Gothic style architecture. Built in 1741, it is one of the last additions to the garden at Stowe formed for Lord Cobham. That same year, "Capability" Brown arrived as gardener, to begin his transformation of the landscape to create one of the finest landscape gardens in the world.

Lord Cobham decided to dedicate his new temple, designed by James Gibbs, "to the Liberty of our Ancestors", for which the Gothic style was deemed appropriate. Triangular in plan, with castellated gables, accommodation and facilities are contained in the three pentagonal turrets with large Gothic windows, decorated with knobbly pinnacles. The rooms are all circular inside, with mounded stone pilasters and plaster vaults. The main vault of the central space is gorgeously painted with heraldry and from the first floor gallery you can start to appreciate the architectural majesty of the building. At the top of the staircase is a belvedere with stone seats offering a fine view of the landscape, now presided over by The National Trust.

The ground floor provides a kitchen in the base of one tower, and modern bath and conveniences in the second – if in rather surprising places. In between is a lounge with a view of the vaulted ceiling. Climbing the stairs encased in the third tower, you reach two double bedrooms – one in each tower, providing accommodation for four.

As might be expected in such a cavernous property, with high vaulted ceilings and solid stone walls, the effect of the heating system is slight – if any. Be prepared to wrap up well for early or late season breaks, or better still, ignore the temperature and just enjoy the amazing surroundings.

TO DO

Stowe's majestic and famous gardens were designed by "Capability" Brown and are recognized as one of the finest landscape gardens in the world.

VISITOR COMMENTS

• *It has proved to the children that the world does not come to an end when there is no telly.*

• *... we are spoiled for the future – surely nowhere in Britain has a view like this.*

• *I'm glad the Gothic Temple exists, so ordinary people can stay in places as extraordinary as this.*

THE HOUSE OF CORRECTION

18th-century former prison

THE HOUSE OF CORRECTION ⑤⑨
Folkingham, Lincolnshire

THE LANDMARK TRUST
Shottesbrooke
Maidenhead
Berkshire SL6 3SW
01628 825925
bookings@landmarktrust.org.uk
www.landmarktrust.org.uk

ROOMS AND RATES
Accommodation for up to four people, although you might find it a little snug around the dining table all at once. Keep your elbows to yourselves! Prices for the complete property are from £260 for a four-night midweek break in January to £879 for a week in July / August. In early and late season, whereas the rooms are cosy enough, you might find the common areas a little chilly.

LOCATION
Folkingham is one of those agreeable places that are less important than they used to be. It has a single very wide street, lined on each side by handsome buildings, with a large 18th-century inn across the top end. The property is a few minutes' walk from the square, where there is a general store, pub and a couple of shops. Check out Stamford, a beautiful town with plenty to see.

THE HOUSE OF Correction occupies the site of a medieval castle where once the moat and earthworks were sited. Planned as a local prison, it was originally intended for minor offenders – the idle (regarded as subversive) and the disorderly. Folkingham had a house of correction by 1611, replaced in 1808 by a new one built inside the castle moat and intended to serve the whole of Kesteven. This was enlarged in 1825 and given a grand new entrance. In 1878 the prison was closed and the inner buildings converted into ten dwellings, all demolished in 1955.

The grand entrance alone survives. It was designed by Bryan Browning, an original and scholarly Lincolnshire architect also responsible for the Sessions House at Bourne. It is a bold and monumental work, intended to house the turnkey, and the governor's horses and carriage. Now it leads only onto a moated expanse of grass – a noble piece of architecture in a beautiful and interesting place.

VISITOR COMMENTS

• *Anyone who doesn't love their stay here needs to be locked up ... the children were particularly taken with the handcuffs.*
• *Alas, parole came too early! An all too short sentence!*
• *What a pleasure to be an inmate!*
• *How charming to find, behind the grand portico, something so elegant and snug.*

APPLETON WATER TOWER

Victorian water tower on Royal estate

APPLETON WATER TOWER 🔟
Sandringham, Norfolk

THE LANDMARK TRUST
Shottesbrooke
Maidenhead
Berkshire SL6 3SW
01628 825925
bookings@landmarktrust.org.uk
www.landmarktrust.org.uk

ROOMS AND RATES
The tower sleeps up to four
people in two double rooms.
Prices for the whole
property are from £380 for
a four-night midweek break
in January to £1,590 for a
week in July / August.
There is a steep staircase
so it is unsuitable for
disabled guests or toddlers
without close supervision.

A PUBLIC-SPIRITED LOCAL landowner offered the lease of this exceptional Victorian tower to The Landmark Trust which, recognizing that there is seldom an opportunity to preserve a functional building like this, let alone one of such quality, mounted a successful appeal.

Designed by Robert Rawlinson, the foundation stone was laid in July 1877 by the Princess of Wales. The ground and first floors were the dwelling for the custodian, with a viewing room above reached by an outside stairway. In typically ingenious Victorian fashion, the flues from all the fireplaces passed through the centre of the iron tank to prevent the water from freezing – original, simple and practical.

The terrace on top of the tank is protected by an ornate cast-iron railing, and as from the room below, there is a view on all sides over miles of wide, open landscape. Here, on this exposed hilltop, you can even see a distant gleam of The Wash.

TO DO

Apart from marvelling at a view normally seen by birds, balloonists and pilots, the estate is an area of great wildlife diversity. The north Norfolk Broads are within reach, as are shingle and sandy beaches. In winter, it can appear bleak – however a crackling fire and a good pub are a time-honoured and satisfactory local remedy.

VISITOR COMMENTS

• *The view from the top of the tower is marvellous and you can see for miles over fields and cottages.*
• *I can vouch for the magnificence of the stars seen from the roof.*
• *Squeals of excitement as we explored the tower.*

CLEY WINDMILL

Historic windmill

CLEY WINDMILL ⑪

CLEY-NEXT-THE-SEA
Holt
Norfolk NR25 7RP
01263 740209
info@cleywindmill.co.uk
www.cleywindmill.co.uk

ROOMS AND RATES

The ground floor includes a circular sitting room where antique furniture and sofas nestle comfortably around a roaring open fire. The beamed dining room, part of the original warehouse built in 1713, has a warm and friendly atmosphere in which to dine. The upstairs rooms and galleries have stunning views over the marshes and the sea.

In great demand as a wedding venue and for house parties, sleeping up to twenty in nine rooms on a B&B basis, it books a long time in advance. You are recommended to plan well ahead, especially for summer weeks – and as much as two years for weddings. Two night stays are required for all but winter midweek breaks. Prices per room are from £120 to £145 for rooms in the mill itself on a B&B basis.

LOCATION

The windmill stands on the north side of the village within walking distance of the excellent shops. It has uninterrupted views over the sea, the salt marshes and Cley Bird Sanctuary, with Blakeney Harbour in the distance. The large walled garden abuts the River Glaven, surrounded by reeds and tranquility.

CLEY WINDMILL DATES from the 1700s, although the tower was not completed until some time later. It is a well-known North Norfolk coastal landmark in a historically prosperous area that was a major East Anglian port for wool and grain. The windmill commands breathtaking views over the salt marshes to Blakeney Point and the sea, while nestling comfortably by the old quay alongside the flint-walled cottages of the village.

It has been accepting guests since around 1921 when it was first converted into a holiday home.

With improvements and renovations over the years, the original mill, old stables and boathouses have been converted into stylish bedrooms or self-catering retreats for independent holidaymakers.

The windmill provides a guesthouse of immense character, charm and comfort and is a fantastic experience to savour.

VISITOR COMMENTS

- *Such a wonderful peaceful place in superb surroundings.*
- *Our stay has been perfect and we couldn't have enjoyed it more.*
- *Don't change anything.*

FRESTON TOWER

Lookout tower of unknown function

FRESTON TOWER 62
Near Ipswich, Suffolk

THE LANDMARK TRUST
Shottesbrooke
Maidenhead
Berkshire SL6 3SW
01628 825925
bookings@landmarktrust.org.uk
www.landmarktrust.org.uk

ROOMS AND RATES
A twin and double bedroom
on the third and fourth floors
provide accommodation
for up to four.
Prices for the whole
property are from £342 for
a four-night midweek break
in January to £1,281 for a
week in July / August.

LOCATION
On the banks of the River
Orwell outside Ipswich,
facilities are few, but walking
opportunities along the river
and towards Pin Mill abound.

NO ONE REALLY knows who built Freston Tower or indeed why it was constructed. The enigma of its existence points most closely to a wealthy Ipswich merchant called Thomas Gooding, who bought the land of Freston Manor in 1553. Further records have yet to be unearthed and archive notes of the area are few. Its crisp brickwork and distinctive blue diapering suggests that it was always intended to be an eye-catching landmark – perhaps as a lookout tower for Gooding's ships, or simply as an extravagant folly – making it one of the first recorded examples. It may even have been built with royal favour in mind, to coincide with Queen Elizabeth I's progress to Ipswich in 1561.

Set in an old and undulating parkland of oaks, sweet chestnut, cedar and beech trees, the architecture and construction is certainly exquisite. There are no fewer than twenty-six windows dotted over its six storeys, arranged in careful hierarchy. Intricate brick mullions and imitation-stone window surrounds no doubt tested the craftsmen of the day – as they have done more recently for its renovation.

The kitchen is on the first floor, with bathroom above. The next two storeys are bedrooms, a twin with double above, sleeping four in total. The sitting room then tops the tower on the fifth floor, to take advantage of unrivalled views of the River Orwell and its handsome modern bridge.

VISITOR COMMENTS

We have enjoyed living vertically for a week – sad to be coming back down to earth.

MARTELLO TOWER

Napoleonic coastal fortification

MARTELLO TOWER ❻④
Aldeburgh, Suffolk

THE LANDMARK TRUST
Shottesbrooke
Maidenhead
Berkshire SL6 3SW
01628 825925
bookings@landmarktrust.org.uk
www.landmarktrust.org.uk

ROOMS AND RATES
Accommodation for up to four people in two rooms. Prices for the complete property are from £381 for a four-night midweek break in January to £1,540 for a week in July / August. Cooking is on an electric hob. There is a solid-fuel stove for extra heating in the sitting room.

LOCATION
Standing at the foot of the Orford Ness peninsula, between the River Alde and the sea, the tower is only a few hundred yards from Aldeburgh. Many visitors bring sailing dinghies.

THIS IS THE largest and most northerly of the chain of fortified towers put up by the Board of Ordnance to keep out Napoleon. Built in the shape of a quatrefoil to house four heavy guns, nearly a million bricks were used in its construction. Although they successfully deterred the French from invasion, in this exposed position the elements still attack. The installation of a purpose-made canopy over the main living space now provides significant protection with an agreeable nautical resonance of sails and canvas, however you should be prepared, during the rougher seas of winter, to expect that sometimes water will find its way inside.

Sensitively restored by The Landmark Trust after it was purchased in 1971, both exterior brickwork and the vaulted interior are maintained to the typical high standards of the Trust.

Choose your companions wisely as the bedrooms are not fully divided, although they are screened from the central living area. Lying in bed, the echoes from the oiled teak floors provide a sense of being in a larger loftier space – yet you will hear your fellow guests as the acoustics are impressive.

VISITOR COMMENTS

• *We will remember the strange acoustics and the fishermen's lights along the beach.*
• *Here you may live with the sea, the wind and rain, sometimes, the light at Orford Ness flashing at night, and Aldeburgh at just the right distance. The stone-flagged battery on the roof, with the mountings of guns and a high, thick parapet for shelter, is a very pleasant place to be.*

THE HOUSE IN THE CLOUDS

Former water tank, in Merrie England village

SYLVIA LE COMBER ⑥⑤
4 Hinde House
14 Hinde Street
London W1U 3BG
0207 224 3615
houseintheclouds@
btopenworld.com
www.houseintheclouds.co.uk

ROOMS AND RATES
With five bedrooms, there is space to easily accommodate ten people in a variety of double and twin rooms. Weekly lets are preferred and the minimum stay is two nights. A week in low winter season is around £1,940, rising to £2,900 in midsummer and for Christmas / New Year, inclusive of all taxes, towels, linen and utilities.

LOCATION
For arrivals by train the nearest station is Saxmundham, 5 miles away, served from London Liverpool Street, changing at Ipswich.

THE HOUSE IN the Clouds was originally intended to provide an adequate storage capacity for a basic water supply for Thorpeness village in 1923. Faced with the difficult task of hiding a rather hideous structure, the engineering team brilliantly disguised it as a house, which from miles around seems to be a cottage lodged 70 ft up in the trees. The supporting steel structure was boarded in to provide unique living accommodation, although for many years the accommodation did not include the very top of the tower, which housed the 50,000 gallon water tank.

In 1977 the use of the tank for storage was discontinued and it passed into private ownership.

As befits a structure that once held near 350 tons of water, the house is very sturdily built. The many tiny windows offer good light and ventilation. Last refurbished in 2002, it provides spacious accommodation for family holidays having five bedrooms, two with double beds, three with twin beds and an additional double sofa bed. Three bathrooms, drawing room, dining room and the magnificent "room at the top" give the finest views of Suffolk.

The five floors are connected by a total of sixty-seven stairs with four landings and five half-landings – resting seats for the less able on each landing. There is an iron spiral staircase on the fifth floor to the upper gallery.

TO DO

Set in an acre of private grounds, the House in the Clouds overlooks Thorpeness golf course, Thorpness Meare and the sea on the Suffolk Heritage Coast. Close to Aldeburgh, Snape Maltings, Minsmere and other bird and nature reserves, Thorpeness village is different from other holiday resorts, staying true to its founder's 1920s wish that it should be "for people who want to experience life as it was when England was Merrie England".

SUGGESTIONS TO CHECK OUT
WHEN YOU CHECK IN

Houseboat Hotels, see opposite page

THE OLD METHODIST CHAPEL ⑤⑥

Built as a chapel in 1888, it was converted into an antique shop in the 1980s before the owners turned it into living accommodation in the 1990s. The reception room was once the original chapel nave and is 45 ft long, 36 ft wide and more than 30 ft high.

• Doubles £75–£90, singles £50–£65. • **High Street,** Yoxford, Suffolk IP17 3E • 01728 668333

• www.chapelsuffolk.co.uk

THE WINDMILL ⑤⑧

Converted specifically to residential accommodation from a disused tower windmill in 1968, this property offers two bedrooms and sleeps four. Available as a self-catering holiday let, it offers fantastic 360 degree views of the surrounding farmland.

Sleeps four, self-catering. From £350 per week in low season, rising to £400–£700 during the summer. • **Barrowden Road,** Morcott, Rutland, Leicestershire LE15 9DQ • 01572 747 000

HOUSEBOAT HOTELS ⑥③

In a location on the edge of the city centre, Ruby and Lily May are comfortably furnished with showers and plenty of hot water. There is also a dining area / lounge with TV and stereo system. Both boats are fully equipped with kitchen facilities should you wish to snack on board.

• Rates are for the complete boat, with Ruby offering accommodation for up to two guests from £75 per boat per night, and Lily May providing two double rooms for up to four, from £95 per night.

• **Houseboat Hotels,** Victoria Quays, Sheffield S2 5SY • 01909 569393 • info@houseboathotels.com • www.houseboathotels.com

NORTHERN
ENGLAND

THE MUSIC ROOM

More intricate Baroque plasterwork than you'll find in any museum

THE MUSIC ROOM **66**
Sun Street, Lancaster

THE LANDMARK TRUST
Shottesbrooke
Maidenhead
Berkshire SL6 3SW
01628 825925
bookings@landmarktrust.org.uk
www.landmarktrust.org.uk

ROOMS AND RATES
Two bedrooms, sleeping four.
Prices for the whole property
are from £159 for a four-night
break in January to £586 for
a week in July / August.

SQUEEZED INTO A little back alley behind The Sun hotel, this 1730s building was originally a summerhouse in the gardens of the hotel. Restoration was a huge undertaking, as access was near impossible and The Landmark Trust needed to buy the buildings on all sides and demolish them to give builders access to The Music Room itself. Such great efforts also necessitated the creation of a pedestrian square to preserve the striking façade and the glazing of the central Ionic arch to create a rather good ground-floor café.

Once you've climbed to the music room inside you suddenly appreciate what an exceptional property this is, as the Baroque plasterwork is hugely ornate and wouldn't be out of place in a royal palace. With a double bed in the main room, the walls are decorated with the muses: eloquence, history, music, astronomy, tragedy, rhetoric, dancing, comedy and amorous poetry; with Apollo over the fireplace. A fruitful goddess with a torch presides over the ceiling. One muse had vanished entirely and was recreated as a modern girl, big and busty, with a cheerful eye; she makes an excellent muse of dancing.

In the attic above, reached by a narrow stair, the Trust made a twin-roomed flat. From there and from the small terrace on its roof there are distant views over Lancaster (including a fine view of the castle from the sink!).

TO DO

Lancaster is a charming town with many secret corners, including some great traditional places such as an old sweet shop (specializing in humbugs – www.humbugsuk.co.uk) and a traditional coffee shop (not a café), J. Atkinson & Co, founded in 1837, which sells a huge variety of custom blends and roasts its own beans daily. It also runs tours in August and September.

FOUR WINDS TIPIS

Tipi experience from North America in Lake District location

KATIES BARN 63
High Thorn Farm
Selside, Near Kendal
Cumbria LA8 9JX
01539 823755
4windstipis@googlemail.com
www.4windslakelandtipis.
co.uk

ROOMS AND RATES
A total of seven tipis are available for couples, groups or family ceremonies and gatherings. The smallest is a 12 ft diameter Shaman tipi suitable for two, while larger 18 ft Little Wolf and 21 ft Crow sleep four to eight. A full week in the Shaman is £250, while six people staying in the Crow is £670 for a full week. Weekend and short-break options are available from £100 in the Shaman to £260 for six for Friday and Saturday in the Crow. Prices are the same all year round, so try not to unjustly penalize visitors restricted to booking trips in the school holidays.

LOCATION
Between Kendal and Barrow-in-Furness on the shores of Lake Windermere.

THE IDEA FOR this family-run business followed a Cornish tipi holiday in 2004. Falling in love with the nomadic tipi traditions, the family decided to bring the experience to their home county of Cumbria. Learning along the way from Native American teachings, family and visitor experiences provide a culturally fascinating insight to a sustainable way of life.

Traditionally tipis or lodges were made from buffalo hide, sewn with heavy seams and laced at the front with wooden pins, however in a concession to modern living, Four Winds Tipis are hand-made from heavy-duty canvas by Wolf Glen Tipis in Scotland. The tipis are erected following the traditional Sioux three-pole method. The construction of the tipi and liner means that they are cosy and warm in winter and offer cool shade in summer. The tipis are fully weatherproofed and have an internal liner, groundsheet, carpet and decorative rugs.

Supplied equipment is comprehensive and includes comfort items such as cushions and airbeds as well as an outdoor fire bowl to sit round in the evenings. The larger tipis also provide a box of toys and books as well as a copy of Native American teachings for background information. Sufficient crockery, glasses and cutlery are provided as well as chopping boards, bowls, pots and pans to use on the gas cooker. Lanterns, a barbeque and charcoal are also supplied. The site has a central toilet block with male and female washbasins and a shower. Although the site has spring-fed water, it is recommended that water be boiled before use, so bring some bottled water for drinking.

BEAMSLEY HOSPITAL

Circular almshouse

BEAMSLEY HOSPITAL ⓦ
Near Skipton, North
Yorkshire

THE LANDMARK TRUST
Shottesbrooke
Maidenhead
Berkshire SL6 3SW
01628 825925
bookings@
landmarktrust.org.uk
www.landmarktrust.org.uk

ROOMS AND RATES
Providing a double, twin
and single room, there is
accommodation for five,
and should you wish, for
well-behaved dogs. Prices
for the whole property
are from £300 for a
four-night midweek break
in January to £1,603 for a
week in July / August.

LOCATION
The nearest town is Bolton
Bridge and the property is a
short walk from the A59, set
back from the main road.

ALMSHOUSES WERE ONCE a familiar part of towns and villages, providing subsidized accommodation to the poor and needy through charitable endowments. Most were nondescript properties providing basic facilities, but the Beamsley Hospital is more unusual. Originally providing accommodation for sick nuns in the 14th century, this circular stone building is set back from the conventional row of dwellings on the main road. Within were rooms for seven women, encircling a chapel through which most of them had to pass to reach their doors, a daily encouragement to piety. Until the 1970s the little community of Mother and Sisters lived here, their lives governed by ancient and ferociously strict rules.

The hospital was founded in 1593 by the Countess of Cumberland, at a time when the poor had only private charity to depend on. Her building is an Elizabethan conceit, alluding both to the six circles, or annulets, on her husband's coat of arms and to the round churches of the Templars. Her daughter, the formidable northern heroine Lady Anne Clifford, added the front range. She also furnished the chapel and, almshouses being by definition conservative places, these fittings survive. Finding the buildings no longer in demand – perhaps as much because of the strict rules as because of the changing social fabric, the trustees offered the property to The Landmark Trust. The front range is let to long-term tenants; and guests can stay in the other. Using its oddly shaped rooms and repeatedly crossing the chapel is a curious experience, bringing you close to the subtle yet vigorous Elizabethan mind.

GUEST COMMENTS
So near to so many places to see we could have stayed here for a month – so we will probably come back again and again.

CULLODEN TOWER

Folly to celebrate defeat of Bonny Prince Charlie

CULLODEN TOWER **72**
Richmond, North Yorkshire

THE LANDMARK TRUST
Shottesbrooke
Maidenhead
Berkshire SL6 3SW
01628 825925
bookings@landmarktrust.org.uk
www.landmarktrust.org.uk

ROOMS AND RATES
With a double and twin
bedroom there is space
enough for four. Prices for
the whole property are from
£449 for a four-night break
in January to £1,607 for a
week in July / August.
The parking is adjacent to
the building. A top visitor
tip is to keep the doors
closed to prevent any heat
you've coaxed from the
stove from shooting up the
stairway and out of the roof.

LOCATION
On the northern edge of
Yorkshire Dales National
Park, Richmond enjoys year-
round tourism. The closest
rail access is Darlington.

STANDING IN SPLENDID isolation looking down on Richmond, the tower was built in 1746 by John Yorke, MP for Richmond, to mark the Duke of Cumberland's defeat of Bonny Prince Charlie. It stands in the park of his long-de-molished house, at the edge of a steep slope above the River Swale a few hundred yards from the town.

Giant windows flood light into the tall octagonal rooms. A twin bedroom and bathroom are on the ground floor leading to a spiral staircase which rises to the mezzanine with kitchen and dining area. Taking the stairs once again, you reach the first floor (lounge area) and second-floor bed-rooms. Keen eyes will note that the carving and plasterwork style changes from Gothic below to Classical on the upper floors. On the second floor you sleep under what must be one of the grandest bedroom ceilings, worth all the sixty steps you've climbed to reach it. These steps are rather more tiresome if you're caught short in the night and need to visit the bathroom on the ground floor.

TO DO

It's difficult to imagine a more idyllic situation, enjoying lovely views from the big windows all around, looking over the trees of this park, with the sight and sound of the Swale rush-ing over the rocks and stones below. With luck you'll have fine weather and chilled wine, as the roof platform is ideal for an early evening view of the surrounding parkland with a glass or two.

Richmond is a decent market town, with a good weekend market and shops for supplies and treats. Britain's most com-plete Georgian playhouse is also in Richmond, with tours Monday to Saturday from 10 am and productions through-out the year.

• *To have a whole tower to ourselves –
along with an unexpected and amazing
roof – was perfect!*
• *The tower is wonderful – like staying
in a large Wedgwood vase ...*

POT-A-DOODLE-DO WIGWAM VILLAGE

Wooden wigwams, tipis and yurts

POT-A-DOODLE DO ⓐ
Borewell Farm
Scremerston
Berwick-upon-Tweed
TD15 2RJ
01289 307 107
info@
northumbrianwigwams.com
www.
northumbrianwigwams.com

ROOMS AND RATES
Each of the twelve
wooden wigwams sleeps
four comfortably.
The two yurts and four
tipis can squeeze in six
people, or four in comfort.
Wigwams are from £29
per night based on two
adults sharing, rising to
£37 in high season.
Children are £8–£10
per night and additional
adults £14.50–£18.50 in
low / high season.
Tipis are £50 per night
based on four sharing.

LOCATION
Situated on the North
Northumberland coast, Pot-
a-Doodle-Do is 3 miles south
of Berwick-upon-Tweed at
Borewell Farm, Scremerston.

WOODEN WIGWAMS AREN'T exactly traditional on the high plains of North America, however Pot-a-Doodle-Do is one of a network of campsites offering these Scottish-designed, all-weather alternatives to canvas. With good weather protection, yet still providing a camping feel, these huts are becoming an increasingly popular year-round option.

All the wooden huts have heaters using metered electricity (bring £1 coins for the meter), and sleep four to five. The site has a central shower / toilet block and a kitchen with cooker, microwave, washing machine, and a selection of pots, pans, crockery and cutlery so you can rely on a hot meal if it rains. The site also offers two insulated yurts, one 18 ft wide and the other 14 ft, sleeping two to four in comfort. Warmed using wood-burning stoves, they are an alternative for those who want more rustic appeal. The site also offers four traditional canvas tipis for those who don't mind putting on a sweater if the morning is cold. In high summer, the tipis are the most authentic option, but if holidaying with young children or early or late season, the wooden huts are a warm, different choice.

TO DO

Outdoor fires and barbeques are a great experience for the family and the on-site shop sells Aberdeen Angus beef. You might also want to book the Finnish BBQ hut – available at a discount for those who buy meat from the farm. Very popular, you are wise to confirm your BBQ booking at the same time as your campsite booking.

The site offers a children's play area, however you are more likely to want to take advantage of Northumberland country and coastal walks. The site is close to sandy beaches, views of Holy Island, the Farne Islands and Bamburgh Castle. Four walking trails, suitable for different abilities, start from the village centre.

LA ROSA

Eclectic eco campsite with nostalgic kitsch touches

LA ROSA 🎵

MURK ESK COTTAGE
Goathland
Whitby YO22 5AS
07786 072 866
info@larosa.co.uk
www.larosa.co.uk

ROOMS AND RATES
The site can accommodate up to sixteen guests in a variety of caravan and camping options. Prices are £27 per person per night, including bedding, gas, candles and firewood. There is a £2 discount if arriving by public transport. Summer peak season bookings require a minimum two-night stay. It's a good idea to bring a torch and wellies, as well as food supplies, but not too much as some of the caravans are a long walk from the parking.

LOCATION
La Rosa is situated at the end of a rural farm track between the villages of Goathland and Egton, about 8 miles from Whitby on the North Yorkshire coast

THIS FANTASY CAMPSITE is full of nostalgia, romance and all things kitsch, camp and bohemian. There are vintage and classic caravans including chrome Romas full of etched glass, a converted truck with wood-burner and a tipi. Each caravan is furnished in keeping with its theme and includes funky decorations, vintage fabrics and kitsch items chosen to make you smile. With a focus on the environment, the campsite is constructed from recycled, reclaimed or simply found objects and this quirky selection is part of the appeal of La Rosa.

Lit by candles and fairy lights, modern power-hungry conveniences are not an option. Night time get-togethers are offered in a beautiful red and white striped circus-style marquee. Showers are in a converted byre, the compost toilet is in an original vintage wooden shepherd's hut and there is an open-air roll-top bath in the orchard area. Candle-lit bathing for two under the stars is something special! The beds are cosy with good-quality futon mattresses, cotton sheets and plump eiderdowns. You'll find that this fantasy location doesn't really need much more than friends and a bottle or two of wine to make an appealing and memorable stay.

"being green does not mean you can't be comfy, have a laugh or eat chocolate cake"

THE WINDMILL HOTEL

Windmill in the centre of town

THE WINDMILL ⑦⑨
Mill St Scarborough
North Yorkshire YO11 1SZ
01723 372735
info@scarborough-
windmill.co.uk
www.scarborough-
windmill.co.uk

ROOMS AND RATES

You can stay on a B&B or self-catering basis in either of two apartments in the windmill itself. Each flat is open-plan, on two floors and is well equipped for a comfortable stay. Sadly, children are not allowed in the top flat at any time. Self-catering prices are from £85–£105 per room per night, plus metered utility charges. Supplements apply for single nights. In addition, the Windmill has nine en suite rooms built around the cobbled courtyard. Standard double and twin rooms are on the ground floor with direct access onto the courtyard. The Premier four-poster rooms are situated on the first-floor veranda. Depending on the type of room and season, rooms are from £30–£45 per adult, including breakfast, based on two adults sharing.

LOCATION

The Windmill is situated in a cul-de-sac off Victoria Road, at the end of Mill Street. Don't drive too fast as a pavement passes over the road and is easy to miss.

THIS 18TH-CENTURY, GRADE II listed windmill is located minutes from the centre of Scarborough. It offers rooms on a self-catering and bed and breakfast basis in both the tower itself and around the cobbled courtyard.

The site has had a windmill on it for around 400 years, and the present structure dates from 1794 when Thomas Robinson was given the authority to build a new mill. The mill stopped grinding corn in 1927 and, although used for storage, gradually fell into disrepair. Saved from developers who applied to demolish the property for a housing development in 1985, an enterprising couple bought it in 1988 with the intention of creating a hotel. The current owners, Angela and Roland, added an upstairs flat to the windmill following their purchase of the property in 1997. The couple have created a pictorial archive in reception, showing the replacement of sails and the windmill dome, as well as the continual maintenance and restoration they have undertaken.

The First Floor flat has a lounge, kitchen and dining area on the lower floor, accessed by thirteen steps from the courtyard. Upstairs there is a double bedroom and bunk beds for children. The Top Flat has an en suite double on the fourth floor, connected to the fifth-floor lounge, kitchen and dining area. The balcony provides 360° views all over Scarborough, ranging from Oliver's Mount, the Castle, the North Bay and more.

TO DO

Owner Roland has a vast collection of toys displayed in cases in the dining and reception areas. The centrally located Windmill is less than 5 minutes' walk from the station, the Stephen Joseph Theatre and the shopping precinct.

SUGGESTIONS TO CHECK OUT
WHEN YOU CHECK IN

HARD DAYS NIGHT HOTEL

This 110-bed hotel in a Grade II listed city centre location pays homage to The Beatles through a variety of original and specially commissioned artwork and photography. The McCartney and Lennon suites are more themed, the latter in white with a trademark white piano.
• Doubles from £170 for luxury rooms and £190 for deluxe rooms.
• **Hard Days Night Hotel,** Central Buildings, North John Street, Liverpool L2 6R • 0151 236 1964
• www.harddaysnighthotel.com

GREAT JOHN STREET HOTEL

This original Victorian schoolhouse has been transformed into a chic townhouse hotel with thirty unique, individually designed bedrooms and suites. Retaining original features such as exposed brickwork, steel beams and old wooden floors, the Old School House has a city centre location.
• Baby-grand rooms from £235 inclusive of tax, but excluding breakfast. • **Great John Street,** Castlefield, Manchester M3 4FD • 0161 831 3211
• www.greatjohnst.co.uk

SPIRE HOUSE

Built in 1903 as a church, Spire House was converted into a B&B in 1997. Guests can choose from three bedrooms, and off-street parking is available. • It is excellent value with double room £58, single £29. • **Bings Road,** Whaley Bridge, High Peak, Derbyshire SK23 7ND • 01663 73319
• www.spirehouse.co.uk

THE FALLEN ANGEL

Newly opened in the Old Elvet area of Durham, this ten-bedroom Georgian townhouse hotel has individually themed rooms and suites. From sitting in the back of a gold Rolls Royce to view movies and eat popcorn in the movie-themed Premiere, to the indulgent luxury of the Russian Bride penthouse suite with views across to the castle,

Raileisure, see below

cathedral and river, there is something to tempt everyone.
• Double rooms from £150. • **Fallen Angel Hotel,** 34 Old Elvet, Durham DH1 3HN
• 0191 384 1037 • www.fallenangelhotel.com

STRAW BALE CABIN
This eco-friendly cabin was constructed using locally grown straw bales.
Using sustainable construction materials, power is provided by wind and solar panels.
• Sleeps two. Weekend hire from £150.
• **Barmby Grange** • Carr Lane, Eastrington, Goole, East Yorkshire DN14 7QN
• 01430 410662 • www.homegrownhome.co.uk

BATS AND BROOMSTICKS
A Gothic-themed B&B
This Gothic-themed B&B has three bedrooms with features including a metal bedstead shaped as a spiderweb, 6 ft Dracula statue, gargoyle figurines and life-size coffins. • Double rooms only £65.
• **Westgrove,** 11 Prospect Hill, Whitby, North Yorkshire YO21 1QE • 01947 605659
• www.batsandbroomsticks.com

THE STATION HOUSE
Offering B&B accommodation within the converted station building,
The Station House has en suite rooms in The Ticket Office, Porter's Room and a refurbished MK1 railway carriage on the platform alongside. Sleeps six in main station building plus an additional five in the railway carriage.
• From £32 per person per night.
• **Station Lane,** Cloughton, Scarborough, North Yorkshire YO13 0AD • 01723 870 896
• www.cloughtonstation.co.uk

RAILEISURE
Next to the Lincolnshire Wolds Railway, these railway wagon styled rooms offer self-catering accommodation with a twist. While not actually restored carriages, they look authentic and blend in with the surroundings of the station sidings site, itself next to a traditional level crossing.
• There are three railway carriages sleeping four, which cost from £279 each for a midweek break in the summer, rising to £299 at weekends. A full week is £469. • **The Old Station Yard,** Station Road, Ludborough, Near Louth, Lincolnshire DN36 5SQ • 01507 363470 • www.raileisure.com

SCOTLAND
& IRELAND

COVE PARK

Artist residences in converted shipping containers

COVE PARK ③
Peaton Hill
Cove
Argyll and Bute
G84 0PE
01436 850 123
information@covepark.org
www.covepark.org

ROOMS AND RATES
Six self-catering cubes in
the shipping containers plus
two pods. Pods cost £100
per night and Cubes £40
on an accommodation-only
basis. The minimum
stay is two nights.

LOCATION
Cove Park is located on the
Rosneath peninsula on the
west coast of Scotland, 1
hour by train or car from
Glasgow. The nearest
town, Helensburgh, is
20 minutes by car.

COVE PARK IS an international centre for the arts and crea-
tive industries. Founded in 1999 by Eileen and Peter Jacobs,
Cove Park's annual programme of residencies enables national and international artists, working in all art forms, to
undertake research and develop new projects. Situated on a
50 acre site overlooking Loch Long on the Rosneath peninsula, near the fringes of Loch Lomond and the Trossachs
National Park, the peninsula is an Area of Outstanding
Natural Beauty.

When Cove Park's residency programme is not in
progress, the self-catering accommodation, created from
steel shipping containers and two grass-covered pods, is
available for private hire. The pods were the original accommodation for the BBC TV series Castaway 2000, relocated
to Cove Park from their original location on the island of
Taransay. The industry standard shipping containers have an
open-plan layout with standard cooking and sleeping facilities inside. They offer a splendid view from the front windows across to Loch Long and the surrounding hills. With
a balcony overlooking a small pond, the containers afford
marvellous views and a different accommodation option for
weekend breaks or longer holidays.

THE MACKINTOSH BUILDING

Charles Rennie Mackintosh designed property

THE MACKINTOSH BUILDING **84**
Comrie, Perthshire

THE LANDMARK TRUST
Shottesbrooke
Maidenhead
Berkshire SL6 3SW
01628 825925
bookings@landmarktrust.org.uk
www.landmarktrust.org.uk

ROOMS AND RATES
Accommodation for up to
four, with nearby parking.
Prices for the whole
property are from £124
for a four-night midweek
break in January to £770 for
a week in July / August.

LOCATION
Comrie is an unfussy
Highland town, with a
bridge over a pebbly river,
a whitewashed church
and a small square, on
the corner of which, right
at the centre of things,
stands this distinguished
and surprising building.

DESIGNED BY CHARLES Rennie Mackintosh, this building dates from 1903–4, when he was doing his very best work. It was commissioned by a local draper and ironmonger, Peter Macpherson, as a shop with a flat above and workrooms in the attics. The Landmark Trust was able to reunite the elements of the property in 1985, following purchase from the different proprietors, including original owner Mr Macpherson's granddaughter. The main room runs into the projecting turret, which gives it an airy feel, and a pleasant view of the River Earn and the wooded hills beyond. At the back is a long garden, reached by a passage from the street.

GUEST COMMENTS

• *It has made us quite determined to find out more about Charles Rennie Mackintosh.*
• *We were especially fond of the bay window– looking out on to the world of Comrie.*
• *The marriage of Mackintosh building to Landmark Trust is a truly happy one.*
• *A delightful flat, a charming and friendly village, magnificent countryside and enough to do and see to last a lifetime.*

THE PINEAPPLE

Stunning, elaborate, eccentric summerhouse

THE PINEAPPLE ⑧⑤
Dunmore, Central Scotland

THE LANDMARK TRUST
Shottesbrooke
Maidenhead
Berkshire SL6 3SW
01628 825925
bookings@landmarktrust.org.uk
www.landmarktrust.org.uk

ROOMS AND RATES
There is a double and
twin room, as well as the
bathroom, in one wing of
the property. Walk outside
to access a lounge and
kitchen in the other wing.
Prices for the whole
property are from £203
for a four-night break in
January to £1,301 for a
week in July / August.

LOCATION
Between Falkirk and
Stirling, near Kincardine
bridge and Airth Castle.

THE PINEAPPLE IS an elaborate summerhouse of two storeys, built for the 4th Earl of Dunmore. Though classical and orthodox at ground level, it grows slowly into something entirely vegetable; conventional architraves put out shoots and end as prickly leaves of stone. It is an eccentric work, of undoubted genius, built of the very finest masonry. It probably began as a one-storey pavilion, dated 1761, and only grew its fruity dome after 1777 when Lord Dunmore was brought back, forcibly, from serving as Governor of Virginia. There, sailors would put a pineapple on the gatepost to announce their return home. Lord Dunmore, who was fond of a joke, announced his return more prominently.

The Pineapple presides over an immense walled garden. This, in the Scottish tradition, was built some distance from the house to take advantage of a south-facing slope. To house the gardeners, stone bothies were built on either side of the Pineapple. These make plain, unassuming rooms to stay in, although you have to go outside to get from one part to the other.

The Pineapple and its surroundings are owned by the National Trust for Scotland. The Landmark Trust took on the lease in 1973 and restored all the buildings and the walled garden, now open to the public. At the back, where the ground level is higher, there is a private garden for guests, with steps leading into the elegant room inside the Pineapple itself.

TO DO

Locally, a major attraction is the Falkirk Wheel – a modern architectural marvel that connects two different height stretches of canal via a giant counterbalanced wheel. Open all year round, this is an impressive feat of engineering to see in action. Further away, but by no means far, is the ancient city of Stirling with its impressive castle.

VISITOR COMMENTS

• *The experience of actually living in such a building is so much more rewarding than merely visiting.*
• *Hooray for the Pineapple, prickly and proud.*
• *Farewell, old fruit!*

WITCHERY BY THE CASTLE

Indulgent and opulent suites in 16th-century property

THE WITCHERY BY THE CASTLE ⑧⑦
Castlehill
The Royal Mile
Edinburgh EH1 2NF
0131 225 5613
mail@thewitchery.com
www.thewitchery.com

ROOMS AND RATES
Rates for the seven suites
include continental breakfast,
taxes, newspapers and a
complimentary bottle of
champagne from £295
per suite per night.

LOCATION
The Witchery is located in the
historic Old Town at the very
top of the Royal Mile, close to
the gates of Edinburgh Castle.
A gilded heraldic metal sign
marks the entrance. Parking
is available in the nearby NCP
car park on Castle Terrace.

ACCLAIMED RESTAURATEUR JAMES Thomson established the Witchery by the Castle in a building at the gates of Edinburgh Castle on the Royal Mile in 1979. Originally built for an Edinburgh merchant in 1595, it now includes the jewel-like Witchery dining room and a collection of totally indulgent and opulent suites on the floors above and in an adjacent historic building.

Frequently booked months in advance, suites are in demand by A-list celebrities.

There are seven suites to choose from – Library, Vestry, Inner Sanctum, Old Rectory, Sempill, Guardroom or Armoury. All are near-theatrical in their furnishings, lavishly decorated and antique-filled with wall-to-wall decadence, Gothic decor and roll-top baths big enough for two!

James is well known for creating amazing dining experiences and now owns four restaurants in Edinburgh, based on the addition of theatrical flair to excellently cooked local ingredients. Located in the most historic part of the building, The Witchery restaurant is rich, warm and atmospheric, its oak-panelled walls hung with tapestries, mirrors and carvings. Spectacular painted and gilded ceilings similar to those at the Palace of Holyrood House celebrate Scotland's links with France in the Auld Alliance, while much of the panelling was rescued from St Giles Cathedral and a Burgundian chateau. Gilded antique-leather screens, polished church candlesticks and opulent red leather seating completes the setting of this magical dining location, which Andrew Lloyd Webber called the prettiest restaurant ever!

COMMENT
• *... an antidote to bland hotels.*

FERNIE CASTLE

Treehouse with adjoining historic castle

FERNIE CASTLE ⑧⑨
Letham, by Cupar
Fife KY15 7RU
01337 810381
mail@ferniecastle.
demon.co.uk
www.ferniecastle.
demon.co.uk

ROOMS AND RATES
The treehouse is available
from £425 on a half-board
basis Monday to Thursday,
rising to £475 on Friday,
Saturday and Sunday. Rates
are inclusive of 1/2 bottle
of champagne, chocolates,
fresh fruit, soft drinks,
biscuits, continental breakfast
and dinner in the castle.

LOCATION
Situated near Cupar in
the heart of the ancient
"Kingdom of Fife".

SET IN A quiet glade 500 yards from 14th-century Fernie Castle Hotel, the treehouse is perched in six lofty sycamores. Guests first glimpse it through the pines, rowans and elderberries, because of the sun glinting on copper roof tiles. It appears to grow out of the trees with the sycamores bursting right through the floor and up out of the roof!

Entry is via a flight of stairs to a fairylight-festooned balcony where double doors with striking stained glass lead you into the bedroom with an elm king-size bed. Furniture is all hand made and you'll also find a flat screen TV, DVD, CD player and coffee maker, plus a fridge full of champagne, chocolates and other goodies.

Climbing up what appears to be the inside of a hollow tree, you emerge into an octagonal bathroom with walls painted twilight blue and a frieze of fairies who flit among trees overhanging pools of water. The ceiling is awash with stars and a pale moon shines onto grazing unicorns, while in the centre sits a huge slipper bath under a chandelier of leaves and flowers.

There are three balconies all with amazing views of the surrounding countryside, and one even has a swing!

TO DO

Fernie Castle is in a superb location for anyone visiting Scotland. This 450-year-old castle can offer all the character of the past with comforts today's visitor expects from a hotel. Situated in 17 acres of woodland with its own loch, there is ample parking space and places to stroll, or just relax.

THE OLD STATION – ST ANDREWS

Themed house and converted railway carriage offering colonial-style suites

THE OLD STATION **90**
Stravithie Bridge
St Andrews
Fife KY16 8LR
01334 880505
info@theoldstation.co.uk
www.theoldstation.co.uk

ROOMS AND RATES
A suite in the railway carriage
costs £130 per night based
on couple sharing facilities.
A standard double room
in the main house is £90
per room per night, and
a deluxe room £100.
All rates include
breakfast and taxes.

LOCATION
Aim for St Andrews and
follow the A917 out of
town. Take the B9131
towards Anstruther at
Brownhills garage. One
mile further on, cross the
humpback bridge over the
old tracks and turn sharp
left into The Old Station.

STEAM TRAINS ONCE travelled through Stravithie along the Fife coastal line, but now all that remains of a once proud line is a single carriage marooned in what was once the old station at Stravithie. Train enthusiasts will realize that this isn't quite true, as the carriage that now sits on the rails at the back of Colin and Fiona Wiseman's property was once electric, and is an intruder from somewhere in southern England. It does not however detract from its transformation into two luxurious double suites, one with kitchen facilities for self-catering and longer stays. Both suites provide good beds with an en suite shower room, lounge and an outdoor deck.

In addition to the railway carriage, six rooms in the main house are available as guest bedrooms, four of them themed. The Garden and Scottish rooms with their tartans and thistle motifs are perhaps expected, but the Oriental and African themed rooms are more of a surprise. With features such as African prints and ceremonial masks, they add character to your stay and provide an alternative for when the carriage is full.

Scottish hospitality is evident in the breakfast taken in the house, which also provides a library for the dreary days when you haven't done well on the golf course. Dinners aren't provided, as after a day of golf you are more likely to be enjoying the hospitality of the clubhouse, or the fine restaurants of St Andrews.

TO DO

You are less than 2 miles from the world centre of golf at St Andrews and actually closer to the town centre than most of the hotels that trade off the St Andrews name. Golf is the central attraction here, with several championship golf courses nearby and regular championship rounds filling the calendar.

THE OLD CHURCH OF URQUHART

Converted church in the Grampian Highlands

PARRANDIER ❷❸
The Old Church of Urquhart
Meft Road
Urquhart by Elgin
IV30 8NH
01343-843063
info@oldchurch.eu
www.oldchurch.eu

ROOMS AND RATES
On a bed and breakfast
basis, a night costs £29
per person based on a
couple sharing, otherwise
a £10 single occupancy
supplement applies.
There is a discount for stays
of three nights or more, as
well as children under 12.
The full Scottish breakfast
is generous and sets you up
for a day of enjoying the
surrounding countryside.

LOCATION
In the Grampian Highlands,
the church is 5 miles from
Elgin near the village of
Urquhart and around 45
miles from Inverness, or
60 miles from Aberdeen
on the A96. There is plenty
of parking in front of the
church and you can request
complimentary pick-up
from Elgin railway station
by prior arrangement.

THE LISTED CHURCH dates back to 1843 and has lost none of its charm in the conversion to bed and breakfast accommodation. With a 70 ft steeple rising above the rural landscape, it stands proud in the summer months and on a clear winter day is a striking landmark. Except for the small village of Urquhart, this is a very peaceful location and perfect for those who want peace and solitude.

With three bedrooms – this B&B also offers the opportunity to rent a self-catering apartment.

There is a small double on the ground floor under the former balcony of the church. Also on the ground floor is a larger en suite family room with a double, single and sofa bed which can accommodate up to four, or form a large suite for two with a coffee table and lounge area. There is also a travel cot for a baby. The third bedroom is a twin on the first floor and offers views out to the garden through arched church windows. There is a separate bathroom opposite the room on the first floor for the use of the twin.

TO DO

"Parrandier", as the church is known, lies at the heart of the "Laich of Moray" in the lee of the Grampian Highlands – which shelter the area from rainfall. This is malt whisky country, and visits can be suggested on booking.

SLEEPERZZZ

Railway carriage hostel

ROGART STATION ❾❹
Sutherland
IV28 3XA
01408 641343
kate@sleeperzzz.com
www.sleeperzzz.com

ROOMS AND RATES
Twenty-three beds from
£12 per person per night
with a 25% reduction for
children under 12 and a
reduction of 10% for those
arriving by train or cycling.
All bedding is included.

LOCATION
Sleeperzzz is at Rogart Station
in the centre of Rogart,
between The Mound and
Lairg on the A839, 55 miles
north of Inverness. There is
ample parking alongside. It is
also on the scenic Inverness–
Thurso / Wick railway line.

There are three railway carriages, two sleeping eight and one sleeping four, plus a 1930s showman's waggon for three – totalling twenty-three beds in all. Sleeping compartments each have two beds. Each carriage has full self-catering facilities, lounge and showers/toilets.

TO DO

For provisions, Rogart has a well-stocked shop, post office, pub / restaurant and garage.

One of the most prominent characteristics of this remote Highland village is the peace and tranquility. Many visitors say it is the perfect place to get away from it all. Bikes are available free of charge to those staying at Sleeperzzz and Rogart is a beautiful area to explore with plenty of sheltered glens, forests, burns and spectacular hill-top views. Fishing is available on the River Fleet.

A trip to Scotland would not be complete without a visit to a whisky distillery. Tours and tastings are available at Glenmorangie Distillery near Tain (18 miles) and Clynelish Distillery, Brora (14 miles).

LOOP HEAD LIGHTKEEPERS HOUSE

Lighthouse views on mouth of Shannon River

LOOP HEAD
LIGHTKEEPERS HOUSE ⑨⑤
Near Shannon, Co.Clare, Ireland

THE IRISH LANDMARK TRUST
25 Eustace Street
Temple Bar
Dublin 2
Ireland
+353 (0)1 670 4733
bookings@
irishlandmark.com
www.irishlandmark.com

ROOMS AND RATES
Sleeping 5, the complete
property may be rented
for a midweek break in
January low season for
€400 in 2008. A full week
in high season (July /
August) is €994 inclusive of
oil fired central heating.

LOCATION
The station is reasonably
remote, although Kilbaha
village with post office,
shop and pub is only 3
miles away. There is a
good road to the station,
with plenty of parking.

LOOP HEAD LIGHTHOUSE station is the major landmark on the northern shore of the Shannon river. The complex is built on a clifftop with 300 degree views of the sea down to Kerry Head and Dingle, across the Shannon and up the Clare coast to the Cliffs of Moher. With Galway Bay to the north and the Shannon estuary cutting deep into the south, the county of Clare is almost a peninsula.

There has been a lighthouse at this important navigational location since 1670. The light was manually operated until 1971, when electricity was introduced to the station. Loop Head Lighthouse was officially fully automated twenty years later.

Guests sleep in a combination of 2 double and a single room in the lightkeepers house (not the light itself), and there is a shower room and two toilets.

The location is fairly remote and it is recommended that guests bring their own drinking water.

TO DO

The surrounding coastline is of a dramatic character with cliffs sculpted by Atlantic storms where rock ledges and caves are home to seabirds, seals and other maritime animals. The peninsula has always been used as a look out - there are numerous pre-Christian forts along the coast and it provides an outstanding spot to see dolphins, whales and seabirds.

Nearby are the cliffs of Moher, a well known destination with spectacular sheer cliff faces where you can look down on the seabirds flying below you from the edge.

There is easy access to Kerry via the Kilmore/Tarbert ferry for those looking to enjoy the countryside, and easy access to the windswept landscape of The Burren.

WICKLOW HEAD LIGHTHOUSE

95 foot navigation beacon

WICKLOW HEAD LIGHTHOUSE 🌐
Dunbur Head, Co. Wicklow, Ireland

THE IRISH LANDMARK TRUST
25 Eustace Street
Temple Bar
Dublin 2
Ireland
+353 (0)1 670 4733
bookings@
irishlandmark.com
www.irishlandmark.com

ROOMS AND RATES
Sleeping 4 in two double bedrooms, the complete property may be rented for a midweek break in January low season for €624 in 2008. A full week in high season (July / August) is €1575 inclusive of electric central heating. Unfortunately, the property is unsuitable for guests who have difficulty with stairs as there are 109 steps to the kitchen on the top floor.

LOCATION
County Wicklow is just south of Dublin and in these rolling granite hills, lies the source of Dublin's River Liffey – used to make Guinness.

THE OCTAGONAL STONE tower known as Wicklow Head Lighthouse was originally one of pair built in 1781 as a distinctive landmark to eliminate the confusion among mariners who wondered if they were at Howth or Hook Head. It is approximately 95 feet high, and still functions as a long established landmark for sailors.

The Lighthouse was originally lit by lanterns each containing twenty tallow candles. However, because they were high on the hill, and often obscured by fog, the towers were not effective and a new lighthouse was built lower down on Dunbur Head.

The original front tower has long disappeared from the landscape, and following a lightning strike to the rear tower in 1836, the lantern was destroyed. The interior was gutted on all floors, and it was decided that the cut stone shell of the tower should be preserved. A new roof was added and the present protective brick dome added in 1866.

The Irish Landmark Trust acquired the lighthouse in 1996, and set about conserving the tower. This involved replastering the internal and external walls, making and fitting 27 windows, wiring, plumbing, flooring and installing a water pumping system. When the stairs and timber floors were in place, 6 octagonal rooms were arranged vertically. Although the rooms are small, they have high arched windows set into walls which are almost a metre thick.

It is a peace seeker's haven with inspiring and refreshing views of the Irish Sea. The landscape and scenery surrounding the lighthouse provide a perfect backdrop for a unique and memorable break. The lighthouse is a truly inspiring place to stay.

TO DO

Well known for walking holidays, County Wicklow is well served with public paths and has a reputation as The Garden of Ireland. As well as nearby Powerscourt House, Gardens and Waterfall, visitors can visit a reconstruction of a prison ship at Wicklow Gaol. Those interested in knitted garments and crafts might wish to visit Avoca Hand Weavers, which is the oldest working mill in Ireland dating from 1723.

The Hill House, see below

CORSEWALL LIGHTHOUSE HOTEL ⑧²

On the west coast of Scotland about 15 minutes' drive from Stranraer, this luxurious hotel offers rooms in a number of different keeper's cottages that surround the still active lighthouse. Since 1815 a light has guided shipping approaching the mouth of Loch Ryan, and its situation provides amazing coastal views over the Irish Sea to the Ayrshire Coast, Ailsa Craig, Isle of Arran, Mull of Kintyre and Northern Ireland. Their restaurant is worth a visit!
• Midweek rooms are from £75 per person per night on a dinner, bed and breakfast basis and up to £140 for largest suite per person in high season, inclusive of a five-course menu.
• **Corsewall Lighthouse Hotel,** Stranraer, Dumfries and Galloway DG9 0QG
• 01776 853 220 • www.lighthousehotel.co.uk

THE HILL HOUSE ⑧³

Mackintosh's domestic masterpiece
Commissioned in 1902 to design a house and everything in it, artistic genius Charles Rennie Mackintosh designed every feature of this house, from its odd-angled and irregularly shaped walls to the toy cupboards inside the former schoolroom where a self-catering flat is now available, offering views across the Firth of Clyde and beyond.
• The flat, for up to six people, is booked via the Landmark Trust.
Prices for the whole property are from £155 for a four-night break in January to £1,215 for a week in July / August.
• **The Landmark Trust,** Shottesbrooke, Maidenhead, Berkshire SL6 3SW
• 01628 825925 • www.landmarktrust.org.uk

LIBERTON TOWER ⑧⑥

With panoramic views of Edinburgh

Just 2 miles from Edinburgh, this 15th- century landowner's tower, was taken over by the Castles of Scotland preservation trust before offering management to The Vivat Trust. Should you wish to climb to the parapets via a ladder from the twin room, you'll be rewarded with splendid views of Edinburgh.

• There are two rooms for up to four people available on a self-catering basis and prices for a three-night break start from £275.
• **The Vivat Trust,** 70 Cowcross Street, London EC1M 6EJ • 0207 336 8825 • www.vivat.org.uk

PRESTONFIELD ⑧⑧

Capturing the same theatrical charm and opulence through which James Thomson established his reputation at The Witchery, Prestonfield provides an out-of-town setting. With manicured lawns, peacocks and another amazing restaurant, this is a gem of an Edinburgh property.

• Doubles from £275 per night.
• **Prestonfield,** Priestfield Road, Edinburgh, EH16 5UT • 0131 225 7800
• mail@prestonfield.com
• www.prestonfield.com

CRAIGHALL CASTLE ⑨①

The only castle in Scotland where you can stay for only £40

Built for the Rattray family in 1533 on a cliff overlooking the River Ericht, Craighall Castle offers two guest bedrooms on a B&B basis.

• Doubles from £70, singles £40
• **Blairgowrie,** Perth and Kinross PH10 7JB
• 01250 874749
• www.craighall.co.uk

CASTLE STUART ⑨②

Castle Stuart, owned by the Stuart family since 1625, has eight guest bedrooms, named after the Scottish clans who fought and died for Bonnie Prince Charlie at Culloden and decorated with their respective tartans. A four-course dinner is included in the price. • Double rooms are £390, no single occupancy.

• **Petty Parish,** Inverness, Inverness-shire IV2 7JH • 01463 790745
• www.castlestuart.com

KILVAHAN HORSE-DRAWN CARAVANS ⑨⑥

Traditional Romany vardos, on a self-drive basis, are a fantastic way to enjoy the relaxed pace of Ireland. After lessons and a first night at the farm (and zoo!), you choose a route with pre-organized stops. The gentle horses know the routes and guide you to your destinations.

• One week from €720. Four-day breaks from €450. • **Tullibards Stud,** Coolrain, Co. Laois, Ireland • +353-57-8735178
• www.horsedrawncaravans.com

KILLIANE CASTLE ⑨⑦

A 13th-century Norman castle with eight bedrooms, the extensive grounds also feature a driving range and golf course.

• Twin and doubles €100, single €75. Family rooms are also available.
• **Drinagh,** Co Wexfor, Ireland
• + 353 53 915 8885
• www.killianecastle.com

SCHOOLHOUSE HOTEL ⑨⑨

Originally opened in 1861 as St Stephen's Parochial School in central Dublin, it lay derelict before being converted to a hotel in 1998. It was refurbished in 2006 with each of the thirty-one rooms named after a famous Irish writer, linking the hotel with its educational roots.

• Double rooms are from €199 per room per night, inclusive of a full cooked Irish breakfast and tax.
• **2–8 Northumberland Road,** Ballsbridge, Dublin 4, Ireland
• +353 1 667 5014
• www.schoolhousehotel.com

ABOUT THE COVER SHOT
The House in the Clouds © Mark Staples
www.markstaples.co.uk

**ALL PHOTOGRAPHS USED WITH KIND
PERMISSION OF THE FOLLOWING:**
Fort Clonque, Nicolle Tower, Beckford's Tower, The Egyptian
House, Lundy, Luttrell's Tower, Hampton Court Palace, Appleton
Water Tower, Martello Tower, The House of Correction, Gothic
Temple, Freston Tower, Beamsley Hospital, Culloden Tower,
The Music Room, The Mackintosh Building, The Pineapple
© The Landmark Trust.
Railholiday, Broomhill Art Hotel, Star Castle Hotel
Seven Degrees West, La Corbière Radio Tower © Jersey Heritage Trust
Sally Port Lighthouse cottage, Wolf Rock Lizard Lighthouse,
Lodesman, Khina Lighthouse cottages © Rural Retreats Limited
Crazy Bear – Oxford, Beaconsfield © Crazy Bear Group Ltd.
Pavilion Hotel, The Old Railway Station, Castle Cottages
Livingstone Safari Lodge, Vintage Vacations, Hotel Pelirocco,
The Enchanted Manor, The Aberporth Express, Caban Casita,
Showman's Waggon, Black Mountain Yurt © Under The Thatch Ltd.
Snowdonia Manor / Plas y Dduallt , Cledan Valley Tipis
Capel Pentwyn, The Citadel, The Lighthouse, Llandudno
West Usk Lighthouse, The Summerhouse,
Liberton Tower © The Vivat Trust
Houseboat Hotels, The House in the Clouds, Cley
Windmill, Featherdown Farm, The Windmill Hotel
Pot-A-Doodle-Do Northumbrian Wigwams, Four Winds Tipis,
La Rosa, The Old Station, Witchery by the Castle, Fernie Castle,
Sleeperzzz, The Old Church of Urquhart, Cove Park, Wicklow Head
Lighthouse, Loop Head Lightkeepers House © Irish Landmark Trust

ACKNOWLEDGEMENTS
Thank you to the many property owners, managers
and photographers who have contributed to this
book. With love as always to our youngest reviewers,
Oliver and Arran. To Geoff Dobson, Simon Penn,
Dan Stride, Jay Christopher, Mike Edwards, Mark
Williams and Lisa Mabbs – thank you for being
there when I needed you most. To contributors and
friends including Ray Mason, Andrea Rademan, Timo
Kiippa, Sharla Ault, Doug Grant, Linda Seymour,
Richard Clarke, Ian Tunnacliffe, Russell and Bob
Strawson – thank you for your honesty and persistence.
Finally, to Sid, Laxmi, Hemant, Priya and the Iniquus
team – thank you for your patience and great work.

ABOUT THE LANDMARK TRUST
Many properties featured in this guide have been
selected from The Landmark Trust, one of the
UK's leading building conservation charities,
with their kind permission. For over forty years
it has been rescuing historic buildings at risk,
giving them new life and a future. Once restored,
Landmarks are let for holidays. The income is
used to support their ongoing maintenance and to
ensure that they will never again fall into decay.
Pricing varies according to property size, season
and length of stay and are for the complete
property only – single room lets in larger
properties are not possible. Contact the office
for latest information, availability and rates.

The Landmark Trust
Shottesbrooke
Maidenhead
Berkshire
SL6 3SW
bookings@landmarktrust.org.uk
www.landmarktrust.org.uk
01628 825925

ABOUT UNDER THE THATCH
Many properties in our Welsh section have been
selected from Under the Thatch – a restoration
project started in 2001 by the immensely likeable
Dr Greg Stevenson. Winner of the Guardian /
Observer Ethical Travel award in 2007, Under the
Thatch restores historic cottages and properties of
interest and, like The Landmark Trust, uses rental
income to support ongoing maintenance and
preservation of traditional building techniques.
Prices vary according to season and property, with
some last-minute holiday discounts available.
Under The Thatch
Bryn Hawen
Henllan
Llandysul
Ceredigion SA44 5UA
01239 851 410
post@underthethatch.co.uk
www.underthethatch.co.uk

CARTOGRAPHY: Cyrille Suss
DESIGN & LAYOUT: Roland Deloi
PROOF-READING: Caroline Lawrence

© JONGLEZ 2009
ISBN: 978-2-9158-0752-3
Printed in France Mame Imprimeurs (08102214)